Al Laney (1896–1988) of the Paris Herald *and the New York* Herald Tribune, *a great newspaperman in his signature outfit: blue serge suit and Borsalino fedora.*

THE CLASSICS OF GOLF

Original Edition of

FOLLOWING THE LEADERS

A
REMINISCENCE
BY

AL LANEY

Foreword by Herbert Warren Wind
Afterword by Carol McCue

For
Michael Laney

Published, 1991, by Ailsa, Inc. by agreement with the copyright holder, The Michael Laney Trust. First Edition.
ISBN 0-940889-34-X.

Foreword

In 1924, Al Laney, a young man from Pensacola, joined the staff of the Paris Herald, *the lively English-language daily newspaper that was a favorite all over the continent. He served chiefly as night city editor, but he filled in at other desks and covered the big tennis and golf championships in Britain, France, and the United States. No other tennis and golf writer moved back and forth across the Atlantic quite the way Laney did, for he was also a member of the celebrated sports staff of the New York Herald Tribune, the rich and powerful aunt of the Paris* Herald. *In the middle 1930s, he came home from France, where he had spent some of the most fulfilling years of his life. (He wrote a fine memoir called "Paris Herald" which continues to be read by many young Americans. It urges them to go to Paris and extend their knowledge of the arts, sciences, and people.) He remained on the sports staff of the* Herald Tribune, *writing tennis, golf, baseball, ice hockey, football, and what-have-you until the late 1960s when the paper ceased publication.*

Laney retired at the time. Not long afterwards he started work on a book that was called "Covering the Court", a fascinating account of his lifelong love affair with tennis. Published in 1968 by Simon & Schuster, it is considered by many sports authorities to be the best book ever written about American tennis. It is mainly about the decade of the 1920s when "Big Bill" Tilden became the greatest player of the day and when the hard-working young French stars—René Lacoste, Jean Borotra, Henri Cochet, and Jacques Brugnon—dedicated themselves to learning how to beat Tilden and capture the Davis Cup. The book also includes a carefully detailed account of the dramatic meeting between Suzanne Lenglen and Helen Wills in Cannes in the spring of 1926.

Laney took a breather after finishing his tennis book and then began work on a lengthy account of his years in golf. He introduced himself in the opening chapter, A Life in Sportswriting. He then went on to recall in detail his boyhood memories of how he had been captivated by Francis Ouimet's victory over the invading British giants, Harry Vardon and Ted Ray, in the historic playoff of the 1913 United States Open at The Country Club in Brookline, Massachusetts. The book went on to cover the early years of Laney's deep and abiding friendship with Bobby Jones, which began in 1919 when Jones was seventeen and Laney, home from France where he had served in the war, was twenty-three. The book included close-up reports on the personalities and skills of such diverse champions as Walter Hagen, Gene Sarazen, Byron Nelson, Sam Snead, Ben Hogan, Arnold Palmer, Ken Venturi, and Jack Nicklaus. Laney mentioned the book occasionally in his conversations with his friends but not at length. In the winter of 1979, we now know, he gave the manuscript to Keith Jennison, a friend of his in publishing, in the hope that Jennison might be able to interest a reliable house in bringing it out. Laney by then was in his eighties and living in a retirement home in Spring Valley, New York. His many friends made certain to drive out regularly and visit with him. Early in the winter of 1988, his mind still wonderfully clear, Al Laney died in his sleep shortly after his ninety-second birthday.

At the time of Laney's death, none of his friends knew what had become of the golf book he had worked on in the 1970s. In 1990, the book suddenly surfaced. Jennison sent a copy of the manuscript to Robert Sommers of the United States Golf Association. Among his other duties, Sommers is the U.S.G.A.'s Director of Communications and the editor of the U.S.G.A.'s magazine, The Golf Journal. *A close friend of Laney's, Sommers sent a copy of the manuscript to Robert Macdonald on the chance that The Classics of Golf might be interested in publishing Laney's unpublished book. Macdonald read the manuscript and was most enthusiastic about it. He then passed it on to me. I felt the same way he did. The Classics of Golf subsequently was able to purchase Laney's golf memoir. We think it is not only a very enjoyable book but a significant one. We have given it what we think is an appropriate title: "Following the Leaders".*

* * *

I don't know for sure what Al Laney's first name was, but I think it was Albert. At any rate, he never used it. His friends got the impression that early in his life he set out, for whatever reason, to make himself into a person of high standards who did first-rate work. He rarely spoke of his boyhood years in Pensacola. One got the feeling that he wasn't very close to his father, a brilliant lawyer who died at a fairly early age. Al didn't mention his mother much either. One gathered that he liked her. Every so often when he was working on the beautifully planted and tended vegetable garden at his summer place deep in the woods of Redding Ridge, Connecticut, he mentioned that his mother was a fine gardener. I believe that, in addition to his brother, Dent, who became a businessman in Fort Worth, Laney had four sisters. One summer I met one of them—I think her name was Willie Lee—at the Laney's summer place. Quite elderly at that time, she was much more Southern than Al and a real chatterer. She was forever going on about how scrumptious certain local fish from the Gulf of Mexico could be when properly prepared.

Laney's wife, Irene, also came from the Pensacola area. A very pretty blonde who was a good deal younger than Laney, Irene had an uncommonly serene disposition. Laney, who usually had a number of things on his mind that he was trying to think through, forever marvelled at how easily she coped with life. He met Irene not long after he had returned from Paris and had settled in New York. She was a talented pianist who had come to the metropolis to continue her musical studies and to teach. Friends in Pensacola asked Laney to look her up. When he first called on Irene to take her to dinner, he was bowled over by her youthful beauty. He never forgot the first words he said to her: "If I had known what you looked like, I would have worn my best suit." Al was forty-two when they were married. Irene soon established herself as a teacher for advanced students and as an accompanist for outstanding musicians in symphony orchestras who also performed in one-man and small group concerts. The musicians she worked with and their families came to be the Laney's closest friends. Michael, their only child, became a professional cellist.

Laney, it should be mentioned, was a handsome man. A person of average height, a bit on the thin side, he had a well-shaped head, straight dark-brown hair, the chiseled features of a movie star, bright blue-grey eyes, and a neatly trimmed moustache. Women loved his looks, his charming low-key manner, and his intelligence.

By the time Laney was married, he had survived several critical illnesses. He rarely mentioned those difficult times and then very briefly. I never learned the real story, but when he was serving as an infantry officer in the Argonne offensive in the closing stages of the First World War, he was badly gassed and spent months in army hospitals before being cleared to return to the United States and civilian life. (He spoke so softly and in such a thin voice that I was often on the verge of asking him if the poison gas was responsible for this, but I never got around to it.) Somehow or other I picked up the story that near the end of the 1920s Laney had come down with a bad case of tuberculosis and had spent many hard months in hospitals near Paris. He came back from that, and in the early 1930s he came back from a scary bout with alcoholism. He was able to give up drinking almost completely. The only liquor he touched during the forty years I knew him was an occasional spoonful of brandy when he was exhausted at the end of a particularly long working day. Later, when we all learned how dangerous cigarettes were, Al, a heavy smoker, was able to give them up. Somehow he found the inner strength to do whatever he had to do to keep in the midst of life. He loved his work—the skillfully played and thrilling sports he watched; his friendships with the athletes and coaches he admired and with the colleagues he enjoyed; and, last but not least, the chance to write an account that, despite a tough deadline and limited space, came close to doing justice to a moving performance he had just witnessed. He was a great newspaperman who was fortunate to live in an era when newspapers were the main means of communication around the world. At the same time, Laney had such a fine mind that he would have been an outstanding writer in any age. He had a gentlemanly, contemplative, clear, and rather English prose style. (When he wrote words or phrases in a series, for example, he followed the English punctuation style and omitted the comma after the penultimate word or phrase in a series.) There was also a certain tone to his writing that suggested the late-nineteenth century approach to life in general.

* * *

What other thoughts come to mind when I think about Al Laney? Well, Al was such a gentle man that you could understand why the birds visited his two-acre place in Connecticut in unusually large numbers and were less skittish than birds generally are. He carried birdseed in the front left pocket of his country jeans. If he was otherwise occupied, the sparrows and other small birds went straight to that pocket and helped themselves. At Augusta National he loved to hear the song of the mockingbirds. Greater numbers of them seemed to be on hand when the Masters was young and comparatively undiscovered. . . .

At about eleven o'clock on the Wednesday morning before the Thursday on which the Masters began, Laney and Ed Miles, the veteran sportswriter for the Atlanta Journal *and an old pal of his, would walk up the hill to the Jones Cabin and visit with Bob. Bob didn't care much where the other writers sat when they called on him, but he always made sure that Laney was seated in the chair closest to him. . . . Laney jumped directly into newspaper work after graduating from high school, but he was a highly educated man. Back in his Paris days, he was one of the volunteers lined up by Sylvia Beach, the proprietress of Shakespeare & Co., the renowned Left Bank bookshop, to read to the elderly James Joyce, who was having trouble with his eyes. . . . I first became aware of Laney when I went away to college in the mid-1930s and started reading the New York newspapers. There was a small headshot of him at the top of his daily reports in the* Trib. *It depicted him wearing a wide, gray, snap-brim Borsalino fedora, a beautifully made Italian hat. He bought a new one each year for decades. . . . I didn't get to meet Al until the summer of 1953 when the biennial Walker Cup match was played at the Kittansett Club, on Buzzards Bay, in Massachusetts. I had dropped him an occasional note telling him how much I had enjoyed something he had written. I always received a very pleasant reply. At Kittansett I introduced myself, and we walked four or five holes together. The next year I joined the staff of* Sports Illustrated, *and after that we saw a good deal of each other. . . . Many things about Laney amazed me, among them his knack for wearing his signature blue serge suit for days on end. Apparently it never needed to be cleaned or pressed. It always looked good. He always looked neat. . . . In those days the Metropolitan Golf Association was a closely knit organization. It was made up—as I believe it is today—of clubs in New York, New Jersey, and Connecticut within seventy-five miles of some spot in central Manhattan. Laney visited many of the top clubs once or* twice each year in the process of covering the big local events or just checking on how the various clubs and certain old friends of his were getting along. He was cherished by the members of many of these clubs whom he had known since the 1930s when the pace of life was slower and people found the time to visit with one another. The annual dinner of the Metropolitan Golf Association was one affair he never missed. He loved catching up with his old friends and his new friends. Al, by the way, got to know talented young golfers like Byron Nelson, Jackie Burke, Jay Hebert, and Shelley Mayfield when they were young fellows getting started at Winged Foot or other clubs in the Metropolitan district.

* * *

As I mentioned previously, The Classics of Golf decided that "Following the Leaders" might be a good title for Laney's manuscript. Laney was not one of those sports writers who spent their days interviewing each other in the press tent or at the clubhouse bar. He loved being out on the course, walking a few holes here and there with players he liked to watch, but, for the most part, following the leaders.

Al was wonderful company out on the course. One incident that I remember clearly took place in 1962 and involved Gene Sarazen, one of Laney's oldest friends in golf. That spring, Gene, who had turned sixty in January, became the first player of that age to make the 36-hole cut in the Masters and, ipso facto, the first to qualify to play the last two rounds of the tournament. On Friday, the day of the third round, I walked with Laney up the first fairway after Gene and his playing partner, Arnold Palmer, had teed off. They had to wait several minutes before playing their seconds, for both players in the twosome in front of them had run into trouble, and it had taken them a fair amount of time to complete the hole. Gene used that interval to scan his gallery carefully and to check on how *many friends of his had actually taken the trouble to come out and watch him on this notable occasion. As he slowly surveyed from left to right the throng standing some forty yards away, his eyes happened to meet ours for a split second. An instant later, Laney grinned and remarked dryly, "The Squire spotted us all right. Now we can leave him any time we want to."*

Most of our golf champions have been fairly impressive young men with pleasant, uncomplicated personalities. A few of them, however, walked to the beat of a different drummer. Ben Hogan certainly did. Laney's chapter on Hogan is the lengthiest by far in his book, because Hogan remained a force in championship golf for so many years. He amassed four victories in our Open between 1948 and 1953 at Riviera, Merion, Oakland Hills, and Oakmont, in that order. What thrilling performances they were! Hogan had no idea of retiring after winning three of the four major championships in 1953. He aspired, among other things, to be the first man to win five U.S. Opens. Laney's meticulously detailed account of Hogan's glorious failure in the 1955 Open at the Olympic Club, in San Francisco—Ben ultimately lost to Jack Fleck in a terse and exciting playoff—is a memorable performance by a very observant writer in top form. So, too, is his account of Hogan's magnificent play in 1960 at Cherry Hills, near Denver. On the seventy-first hole of that championship, Hogan, tied for the lead, did something he always said he would never do: he elected to gamble on pulling off a terribly risky shot on which the winning of a major championship might very well depend. It was a touchy little wedge pitch over water to an island green on which the pin was set unusually close to the hazard. Ben's gamble failed by inches. The ball caught the very top of the far bank of the hazard and dropped down into the water. This climactic episode in Hogan's last bid to win a fifth U.S. Open had the inevitability of Greek tragedy. The gods simply would not countenance a mortal's insolence in trying to pull off the kind of miracle the gods reserve for themselves.

Laney's portraits of Arnold Palmer, Ken Venturi, and Jack Nicklaus are also exceptional because of his insight into these very different men. He is able to put into words how it was that Arnie, the handsome boy next door, was able to communicate in such an amazing way with his idolatrous fans. There may never again be such faithful and adoring galleries as the ones that made up "Arnie's Army" wherever he played. Certainly no one who was present will ever forget the cameo incident that took place on the second round on the par-3 sixth hole of the Bellerive Country Club, in St. Louis, in June, 1965, when the club was host to the U.S. Open. A massive gallery, a dozen rows deep in spots, surrounded the green after Arnold had put his middle-iron tee shot about twelve feet from the hole. There was complete silence as he lined up his putt for the birdie and tapped the ball towards the hole. There were all varieties of moans and groans as the ball edged by the cup. Then the stillness was broken by a woman's voice saying, "Oh, Arnold. Really!" She was a nice-looking, middle-aged lady, and one would have thought from her intonation that she had known Palmer all his life. Laney captures the moment perfectly. For that matter, no one has ever explained as clearly as Laney Palmer's astonishing ability to communicate so naturally with the men and women of all ages and backgrounds who made up "Arnie's Army."

Laney understood the young Ken Venturi much better than most people did. As you may remember, Venturi threw away the chance of a lifetime in the 1956 Masters. Twenty-five at the time, his military service behind him, the highly-touted amateur from San Francisco entered the final round of the Masters tournament with a seven-stroke lead on the nearest man, but he played a jittery 80 and eventually ended up a shot behind Jack Burke, Jr. A good many old sports hands had an idea that we might have seen the last of Venturi, but he surprised a lot of people. After turning professional late in 1956, he grew up into a mature and enjoyable man. He worked hard on his game and soon became one of leading players on the pro tour. He soon came to be recognized as one of the finest iron-players of the day, and many students of the game considered him the most talented long-iron player they had ever seen. (He could hit the ball right-to-left or left-to-right, high or low, or on whatever parabola the lay of the land, the weather conditions, or the position of the pin suggested.) Suddenly, he was plagued by a series of strange and seriously debilitating ailments for which his doctors could find no remedies. He bravely stayed out on the tour, but his game steadily disintegrated. On top of this, he was harried by new ailments that also baffled the specialists. Ken hung on as best he could, and he never complained. His courage won him the lasting respect of his colleagues.

Early in the spring of 1964, Venturi started to regain something of his old form. He finished near the top in several tour tournaments. He qualified handily for the U.S. Open, which was held that year at the Congressional Golf Club, outside Washington, D.C., during a fierce heat wave that reached its peak on the Saturday when the last two rounds were played. In the third round, Venturi hit a succession of superlative shots, and his 66 brought him to within two strokes of the leader. However, the heat had gotten to him on the fourteenth hole, and he was near collapse when he reached the clubhouse. He had nothing for lunch except a cup of tea. The doctor who attended him during the fifty-minute break between rounds gave him some salt tablets to take and walked out on the course with him in the scorching heat of the after-noon round. Venturi managed to continue to play bril-liant golf. On the fourteenth hole, however, his step began to falter and his eyes began to look glassy. He managed to keep going, somehow or other, and at length came stag-

gering down the long, hillside fairway that led to the eighteenth green. He finished the long day by playing a daring bunker shot onto the dangerous home green and then proceeded to hole a tenfoot putt for his par, a round of 70, and a four-shot margin over the runner-up, Tommy Jacobs. The gallery really let the new champion know how they felt about his courageous performance.

Ken Venturi proved to be much more than a three-days wonder. He went on to play excellent tournament golf for many more years. He became one of the most sought-after teachers in the country. He and his friend Pat Summerall came to be recognized as the top team of golf announcers on television. His private life has been a happy one. Along the way, Ken also gained a reputation for being a man who somehow could help people with serious problems when everyone else and everything else had failed.

Last but not least, there is Laney's portrait of Jack Nicklaus. Nicklaus accomplished so much so quickly in tournament golf—for example, he won his first U.S. Amateur in 1959 at the Broadmoor Golf Club in Colorado Springs, south of Denver, when he was nineteen; led the United States team to victory in the second World Amateur Team Championship at Merion, outside Philadelphia, in 1960, when he was twenty, with rounds of 66, 67, 68, and 68; won his first U.S. Open at Oakmont, near Pittsburgh, in 1962 (after a playoff with Palmer), when he was twenty-two; won the first of his six Masters titles in 1963 when he was twenty-three; won the first of his five P.G.A. Championships at the Dallas Athletic Club also in 1963; and won the first of his three British Opens at Muirfield in 1966—that it is hard to remember him as anything but the strong, confident young man who was more at home out on the course, surrounded by thousands, than most of us are in the privacy of our living room. Jack had an exceptionally close relationship with his father Charlie, a wonderful man. (Charlie Nicklaus had played professional football under an assumed name for the Portsmouth Spartans of the National Football League to help pay his way through the College of Pharmacy at Ohio State University.) At the same time, like any young man, there were quite a few things that Jack Nicklaus was unsure of and even somewhat concerned about, and he found that Laney was one sportswriter with whom he felt very much at ease. They enjoyed many pleasant conversations down through the years. As a result, Laney writes of the young Nicklaus in his various stages of development with far more perceptiveness than any other writer I can think of. The only exceptions would be the two golf writers for his hometown papers, Kaye Kessler, of the Columbus Citizen-Journal, *and Paul Hornung, of the* Columbus Dispatch. *Both were devoted friends.*

Jack Nicklaus, as we all know, went on to compile the finest record of any golfer in the history of the game. At the present time, he has won a total of twenty major championships: six Masters, in 1963, 1965, 1966, 1972, 1975, and 1986; five P.G.A. Championships, in 1963, 1971, 1973, 1975, and 1980; four U.S. Opens, in 1962, 1967, 1972, and 1980; three British Opens, in 1966, 1970, and 1978; and two U.S. Amateurs, in 1959 and 1961. Laney was very much on hand when Jack won the 1967 U.S. Open at Baltusrol. After that, thanks to television, he was able to watch Jack's subsequent victories in the major championships. The last of these came in the 1986 Masters when Jack overtook and passed the leaders with a really phenomenal rally down the stretch on the fourth day. I saw Al not long after that, and he was still filled with fervor when he spoke of the great shots that Jack had been able to bring off when he had to. I doubt that as a boy in Pensacola in 1913 he could have been more thrilled when the news finally came through that Francis Ouimet had defeated Vardon and Ray in their playoff for the U.S. Open at The Country Club.

* * *

As you will discover in this memoir, Al Laney was both a romanticist and a realist, the first by inclination, the second through experience. A student of human nature, he knew who were the princes and who the pretenders among both the well-born and the working stiffs. He had an intuitive understanding of those rare people with good hearts and good heads whose lives are based on high standards and the spark of life. Some of these persons, like his great hero, Bob Jones, were at one time or another beset with deep emotional problems that threatened to wreck their careers and their lives. (His long friendship with Jones was of inestimable importance to both men.) Though somewhat shy and physically delicate, Laney was tough. He had the hardiness to get through long, lonely stretches by himself, if he had to. From the beginning, he meant to lead the richest, fullest life possible, and, as he grew older, the knowledge that he had managed to realize a fair number of his aims and desires made him happy and strong. The best part of his life had ended when Irene came down with an incurable cancer in the late 1960s and, after a fairly long illness, died in a cancer clinic across the Hudson River. Characteristically, she never complained and remained sunny and serene to the end. During the day, Al would sit in her room in a chair at the foot of her bed and work on his tennis book. He needed desperately to have something that would occupy his mind during this hard period. His inner strength sustained him after Irene's death. When I would go up to visit him in his retirement home in Spring Valley, he never seemed old to me. He read a lot and continued to do some writing—good writing. Many of his friends kept in close touch. Whenever I drove up to see him, we would go out for a good steak. Al was the same as ever—bright, cheerful, animated, and full of interesting thoughts. He ate like a young man. One day in early January in 1988, I called him from New York and another voice answered the phone.

Carol McCue, a good friend of Al Laney's and a leader in golf in the Chicago area from the Second World War on, has provided a thoughtful Afterword to "Following the Leaders". Carol was born in Chicago, the daughter of Ethel Sullivan, a fourth-generation Chicagoan, and Jack McCue, the midwestern representative of the Russell Erwin Company of New Britain, Connecticut, which manufactured hardware for the contractors who were putting up the huge new building in our cities. Carol attended De Paul University, in Chicago. Since she took shorthand, a local employment agency sent her in June, 1942, to the offices of the Chicago District Golf Association, the affiliate in that area of the United States Golf Association. That year, with the national golf championships cancelled because our country had entered the Second World War, the U.S.G.A. decided to put on the Hale America Golf Tournament at the Ridgemoor Country Club, in Chicago, with the proceeds to go to the Navy Relief Society and the United Service Organization, the U.S.O. Ben Hogan won the tournament with a four-round total of 271 (72-62-69-68), three strokes in front of Jimmy Demaret and Mike Turnesa. Bobby Jones, then forty years old, played in the tournament's Old Guard division and brought in rounds of 70, 75, 72, and 73. Jones was the main attraction for the galleries, and certainly for Carol. He played excellent golf for a man who had retired from competititon a dozen years earlier.

At Ridgemoor, Carol was responsible for keeping the official daily attendance and other statistics. After the tournament, no one said anything to her about leaving, and she continued to report daily to the downtown headquarters of the C.D.G.A. The men who worked for the C.D.G.A. gradually went off to war. "For a long while, I was the only inhabitant of the office," Carol remembers. "Near the end of the 1940s, I hired a couple of people to *help out. The Chicago District functioned pretty well in its small supporting role when the U.S. Open was held in 1949 at Medinah, about twenty miles from The Loop. That was the year Cary Middlecoff broke through and won his first major title." By this time, Carol was on her way to becoming a fairly good golfer, a solid 10-handicap player. With her excellent mind, pleasant manner, and good looks, she was also well on her way to becoming a local institution. Her administrative ability made her extremely popular with the people who ran the wonderful old private golf clubs in and around Chicago. A child of the times, she also became involved in the dramatic growth of superior public golf courses in the Chicago area in the 1950s and 1960s. (This was particularly true of Cog Hill No. 4 and the other excellent public courses that Joe Jemsek was developing in the town of Lemont to the southwest of the city. Carol also became a favorite of Charlie Bartlett, the longtime golf writer of the Chicago* Tribune *and a local institution; Francis Power and Tom Siler, two really fine men who for many years wrote beautiful stuff about golf and the other major sports; and Herb Graffis, who, with his brother Joe, founded and published the game's leading trade magazines in this country and, with his rampant wit, reigned for decades as the country's most dazzling after-dinner speaker on the big golf occasions.*

I met Carol in 1959, I think, when she was working on something completely new in golf. That year she arranged for a large passenger plane to transport some sixty-five members of C.D.G.A.-affiliated clubs down to and back from Augusta, Georgia, where they watched the golf on Friday, the second day of the Masters. They started home only after they had learned which players had made the 36-hole cut. By 1961, jet planes were available, and two large planeloads of C.D.G.A. golfers made the round trip to Augusta, one on Thursday and one on Friday. These flights to the Masters still continue, and they now run on

Friday with one hundred and forty-eight golfers aboard. (It was on one of these trips to the Masters that Carol got to meet Al Laney.) When the major airlines later made special charter flights overseas available to bona fide clubs and associations in the autumn and winter, the members of clubs affiliated with the C.D.G.A. descended on Europe in hordes for many years. During this period, incidentally, the C.D.G.A. was one of the first golf organizations to make health insurance available to the office staffs and course-maintenance crews of its affiliated clubs, and it also became the first association to calculate handicaps by computer.

In the early 1970s—her parents were gone by that time—Carol began to treat herself to a trip to New York in the autumn to see the outstanding plays and musicals. Some years she went over to London and took in as many of the season's hit shows as she could get tickets to. She started to spend a stretch of the winter with friends in the Miami Shores area of Florida. Exerting tremendous self-discipline, she managed to slow down a bit, went to the race track at least once a week, and generally took it easy. Her friends were shocked, however, when she resigned her post as Executive Director of the C.D.G.A. in 1982. She thought she would like to travel the world, but she discovered rather quickly that she missed working, terribly. She did not return to the C.D.G.A., however, but went to work for her old friend Joe Jemsek as Vice-President of Jemsek Golf. Cog Hill No. 4, which Dick Wilson and Joe Lee designed, had earlier been selected to host the U.S.G.A.'s National Public Links championship in 1970 and again in 1989. The year 1990 turned out to be a significant one for Jemsek Golf. For some time, the Butler National Golf Club, in Oak Brook, Illinois, a club exclusively for men, had been the home of one of the country's oldest tournaments, the distinguished Western Open championship. In 1990, Butler National, rather than changing its structure by taking in women members and

thus complying with the requirements that the P.G.A.
Tour had set for all golf clubs which host the weekly tour-
naments on its annual coast-to-coast trek, decided to step
down as the venue of the Western. A good many golf clubs
in the Chicago area were interested in putting on the tour-
nament, but Cog Hill No. 4 was selected to be the site of
the $250,000 1991 Centel Western Open. In the winter
and spring of 1991, Carol McCue, the new Tournament
Chairman of the venerable championship, had, for once,
enough work to keep her busy for a while.

Herbert Warren Wind

FOLLOWING
THE
LEADERS

FRANCIS OUIMET
WALTER HAGEN
BOBBY JONES
GENE SARAZEN
BYRON NELSON
SAM SNEAD
BEN HOGAN
KEN VENTURI
ARNOLD PALMER
JACK NICKLAUS
AND THE OTHER GREAT
  AMERICAN GOLFERS

TABLE OF CONTENTS

CHAPTER I
A Life in Sportswriting

In the course of a long newspaper career on both sides of the Atlantic I have had the good fortune to be present at more big sports events than most men. Deliberately choosing to pass many years of a no doubt insulating happiness in pursuit of games playing, I covered all major and most minor sports for the lamented New York *Herald Tribune* and other papers for nearly half a century.

When the Ivy was brightly green and the Big Three were lords of football creation, I froze through many an autumn twilight pecking with numb fingers at a primitive portable in primitive press boxes. I sat in indecent comfort at mid-Western pigskin gatherings when the Big Ten was truly big and the Army-Navy game, once the biggest of all, provided many a memorable occasion for extra-curricular activity with splendid companions. I literally lived and figuratively died with the New York Giants when professional football was young, and I have known them and others of their breed after pro football became the biggest thing in sport, perhaps the biggest thing in American life.

The horse racing parks from Belmont, Saratoga, Hialeah, Louisville, and Santa Anita to Epsom Downs and Ascot in England and Longchamps in Paris all have known me on their great days. I travelled the baseball training trail in springtime with the New York Giants, and suffered with the faithful at Ebbets Field. I accompanied the swashbuckling Yankees of Murderers Row on boisterous trips and I knew them as well in the golden autumns of their World Series heroics and excesses.

At many a championship fight my eyes have looked level across the resined canvas, or that part of it not occupied by a comatose heavyweight, and for decades on end no tennis championship at Wimbledon, Forest Hills, or Roland Garros in Paris, and no Davis Cup Challenge Round was conducted without my assistance. At Meadowbrook, Roehampton and Hurlingham I mingled with the Milburns, the Hitchcocks, and the Bostwicks of the polo set when that game was "in". The yachting set at Newport and Cowes knew me, too, and when Adolf Hitler turned the Berlin Olympics into a monster Nazi festival, I was there to observe and to report.

All these experiences and many others I count as blessings, for I am sure there can be few more pleasant ways of earning a modest living than that of an international sports reporter, especially during those decades of uneasy peace between the two World Wars. Now, looking back across the years, I put pleasant memories of these to one side. I now feel that if so great a portion of one's time in life is to be devoted to the playing of games, to watching them, writing of them and their practitioners, then golf, which also has long been my beat, is the best game to choose.

At any rate, it has been the most enjoyable game for me, and I place it first without disparagment of other sports favored by talented observers who have written enduring pieces about them. I have many reasons for my preference.

Golf reporting takes you to lovely places no other sport can match, each place different and likely to be more beautiful than the last. It brings you into more or less intimate relation in pleasant surroundings with more interesting people than any other game. Most of them are intelligent and cultured men and women often of high achievement in other realms of life. The leading figures in golf have been as colorful and interesting as any sport can offer, and, everything considered, the game itself is one of the very best of all "writing" sports.

Baseball parks vary little one from another and a steady diet of baseball reporting becomes, scenically speaking, just a succession of similar press boxes and similar hotels in towns that after a while run together in memory. All famous tennis places, horse parks, and other homes of sport are not, to be sure, identical. A few surroundings have an appeal of their own, and all, in a sense, are hallowed by the great stars who performed there. But the grounds where they compete, where the issue is joined, are all structured the same and have in themselves no distinguishing charm or virtue. Golf, on the other hand, is the most favored of games in the sites where it is played. Golf takes place in "large and glorious places", not on a limited patch of ground. It can be played anywhere: in the mountains; at the seashore; "by the stream and o'er the mead"; through somnolent valleys and over crowded pastureland surrounded by noisy suburban dwellings; and on the silent desert. The extent and form of a golf course lie in the nature of the terrain. You never find two courses exactly alike. Memory enshrines the finest places where we have played golf or seen it played. It is doubtful that many have been enchanted by a basketball court or a football field. Golf induces a feeling for places, often investing them with personality. It promotes an active interest in the outer physical world, and, it seems to me, it satisfies a certain need to love the earth itself.

I enjoyed writing about other sports, especially baseball, a resourceful and ever stimulating game, before the coming of expansion and jet travel that jerks you back and forth through time zones at the speed of sound. But from the start, or very nearly so, I think I enjoyed golf more. It is a pastime of continuing interest as a subject written or oral, and exactly at this period when speed and violence seem to have intoxicated the world, this leisurely game has itself captured new millions of enthusiasts.

Sport lends itself to shallow sentiment, and golf is not immune, but a golf course is one of the last strongholds of disciplined pleasure and courtesy. This game differs greatly from others in which success may be gained only by playing them faster and faster, for it leaves undisturbed the dignity of the participant. And while golf requires the true eye and steady nerve demanded by bat-and-ball games, it eliminates the advantage of superior physique. It is a pastime that suits the physical limitations of the many. In nearly all other games our pleasure as spectator is in watching things being done much better that we could ever hope to do ourselves, and therein lies one of the basic charms of golf. Even the greatest of golfers does nothing that even the least of us has not done at one time or another. All who watch the great ones have holed preposterously long putts and made remarkable recovery shots. And who among us has not now and then caught hold of a tee shot just right and experienced the supreme muscular thrill of a long straight drive? We do these things rarely or, at best, only occasionally, whereas the experts do them all in the course of a round. However, we have permanent memories of certain shots played with professional perfection. It is thus from the analogy of our own achievements that we view the skills of the champion players.

Golf has attracted many famous literary figures, some of whom have written extensively about the game. Among them, I remember A. A. Milne for a remark he made that golf is "the most wonderful game in the world at which to be bad." At any rate, it all began for me one sultry afternoon just before World War I. As a result of having been born shortly before the turn of the 20th century in Pensacola, Florida, I was walking down Palafox Street in mid-afternoon on September 20, 1913, toward what it may be permissible to call a rendezvous with destiny.

CHAPTER II
September 20, 1913

Thousands of dripping rubber-coated spectators massed about Ouimet, who was hoisted to shoulders while cheer after cheer rang out in his honor. Excited women tore bunches of flowers from their bodies and hurled them at the youthful winner; hundreds of men strove to pat him on the back or shake his hand.—From the *New York Times*, Sept. 21, 1913.

If I lived a thousand lives I should never again be spectator to such an amazing, thrilling and magnificent finish to a championship. . . . You tell me that a child like this has beaten our Vardon and Ray for a real championship? When we can go for week-end golfing trips to Jupiter and Mars, I will perhaps believe that your little Ouimet has won today. There will never be another like it. When we are old men little golfing children will ask us to tell them again the romantic story of the 20th of September in 1913.— Henry Leach, English golf correspondent, writing in the *New York Times*, Sept. 21, 1913.

There had been rain that Saturday in Brookline, Mass., but the day was hot and humid 2,000 miles away in Pensacola, and a faint lazy breeze came in off the Gulf of Mexico. About the time the scenes described above were unfolding to astonish, delight, and dismay, I, a teenage lad, was making my slow way through the heat toward the office of the Pensacola *Journal*, to which I had been apprenticed for after-school and Saturday-night service.

I wore, more than likely, the common uniform of the teenager of the day—flat, peaked cap; straight, tapered pants ending just below the knees; home-made cotton blouse with tight neckband for collar; long, ribbed black stockings held up by elastic bands; and either high-laced shoes or white sneakers called easywalkers. Knickerbockers for boys were just coming in, and I stopped to admire a suit in the window of White and White's store. It was a beautiful grey suit with a belted Norfolk jacket, but the tag said $10, an enormous price that I knew was forever beyond me. Only a few of these suits with knickers had appeared in the town or in school, and most boys of my acquaintance would jump right over knickers into long pants, the badge of manhood if not of maturity. I was, in fact, already saving up to buy my own first pair of long pants.

Under the overhanging balconies and upper stories of the building that shaded the sidewalks of the main street and gave an effect of a covered arcade, it was a little cooler, and my dawdling progress would have seemed aimless to an observer. There were few to observe, however. As I dawdled, I wrestled with a puzzle to which I was not to find the answer for many years. Why, I wondered, was I giving up a rare and precious free afternoon? Saturdays were grand, the only completely free time when I was really on my own, since all the news sources I usually checked after school were closed. The time could have been devoted to any number of pleasant schoolboy pursuits, such as sailing a boat, exploring any one of the many inlets and bayous off the harbour, or swimming at Bayview Park where many boys and girls gathered for fun and games. Actually, this particular Saturday afternoon had been set aside for a long, uninterrupted session of tennis that I had anticipated eagerly.

I could explain to myself no more than to my deserted companions why I had to disrupt our plans. They thought I'd suddenly gone strange, for they did not at all understand why I was leaving them in the lurch, reducing four to three and disrupting a carefully planned schedule of alternating singles and doubles play. Tennis partners were not so easy to come by at that time, and after the

start of school I was available only on Saturdays. It
seemed crazy to them and a little that way to me, too.

I tried to explain, but I could not tell them because I did
not know why overnight it had become so terribly important to me to know what was happening in Brookline,
Mass., and why I was driven by this necessity to know the
outcome of a largely unfamiliar game played so far away
by characters whose very names I had not known a few
days earlier.

Much the same thing that had happened to me was
happening to many others in many cities and towns on
that Saturday afternoon, but I was not to know of this
until long after. A certain compulsion, no doubt a certain
destiny, was at work here. I was troubled by a vague
uneasiness, a feeling almost of guilt or wrongdoing, as I
moved slowly through the heavy shade with the brilliant white light just beyond in the street. Once you set
yourself to remember such a special occasion, it all
gradually comes back—the look on the faces of people
you met; individual gestures; what you thought at the
time; what somebody said; the hollow clop, clop of
horses' hooves on the brick pavement; the faint hissing of
ceiling fans, with blades as big as airplane propellers,
inside the wide-open fronts of the stores; the distant
screech of trolley wheels turning from Palafox into
Wright Street half a mile away.

I had progressed as far as Romano Street when I saw
coming toward me Mr. Sheppard, a kind, gray man who
had a drugstore full of fascinating smells way down below
Zaragosa Street on the edge of what was called the Red
Light district, much frequented by sailors from ships in
the harbor. Mr. Sheppard, a well-educated man and
something of an intellectual in a community rather barren
of culture, had been a good and stimulating friend of my

late father, and I knew he would ask me where I was going. I knew, too, that he would not understand, and if there had been time before he saw me, I would have ducked to avoid encounter and question.

"What you doing downtown on Saturday, Boy?" he demanded to know. Mr. Sheppard never called me anything but Boy, even after I put on long pants. The reply that I was going to the newspaper office brought a "What for?", and my further explanation that I wanted to know if Ouimet had beaten the Englishmen brought a puzzled expression to the druggist's face.

I pronounced it "We-May". I was in high school and taking French, and it was not until years later that I learned that the name was pronounced "We-Met", accent on the first syllable.

"What in thunderation are you talking about, Boy?" Mr. Sheppard said, and the attempted explanation sent him on his way chuckling with amusement over school-boy aberrations.

I leaned against an iron column supporting a balcony and thought about this reaction as I watched a round watering cart pulled by two mules. Its two arched umbrella-like jets spurting out behind sent up little gusts of smoke as the water hit the dirty roadway and ran in dusty rivulets. Did anyone else care about what was happening at Brookline? Was it perhaps a little odd to care so much?

Behind the cart came one of the town's curiosities named Leopold in one of those old seagoing hacks that were the only means of public transport other than the trolley lines. Leopold also was a friend, and he called to the driver to pull up to the sidewalk, which was raised about two feet above the roadway. Leopold wanted to tell me how things were going down at City Hall, where they humored him with a desk and a large bunch of keys fitting nothing, and he did nothing to disturb the illusion that he was running the city. He kept regular hours there, riding back and forth in an open hack whatever the weather, bowing and lifting his hat to everyone as a prince to his subjects. He belonged to one of the first families and was a rather charming and harmless man of indeterminate age.

Leopold was of the opinion that chicanery was continually on the prowl and but for his own watchfulness would conquer. He could not distinguish between man and teenager and, since I gave him contact with the power of the press, he looked upon me as a personage of almost equal importance with himself in this community. Together we would overcome the rampant forces of evil. On my daily calls to City Hall he would give me vague information of corruption in high places and direct me to "put it in the paper". Since he could not read, he always assumed that it had been done. Leopold and I enjoyed a very solid friendship. He understood instantly why I was going to the shop so early. His world was either black or white and nothing puzzled him. He was a completely happy man, never angry, always smiling even when misguided small boys would tease him. He gave me a blessing which cheered me greatly and bade me hurry lest I be late.

I paused a bit before the wide open front of an oasis called the Kandy Kitchen where my closest and dearest schoolboy friend, Dwight Anderson, would be thumping out popular songs on the piano for the late Saturday afternoon crowd before moving on to render the same service at the town's one picture show in a vacant store down by Government Street. He was going to conquer the world as musician, I as writer. It also gave me comfort to know that Dwight would understand about this Saturday afternoon, although sports subjects did not move him in the way I thought they should.

I had about decided to go inside for a nickel's worth of cooling drink when a shout from the street made me turn.

"Hey! Where you going? Come on and ride around East Hill."

This invitation came from the only passenger on an open street car with seats running crosswise, a boy who sat just behind the motorman. This was Ralph Scholls, called Gus, a boy of my own age who was coming from somewhere down by the waterfront where there were fascinating things to attract teenagers. Gus was the best roller skater in the whole town, and he had jumped off a picnic boat in the middle of the bay that same summer to save a girl who had fallen in. They said he was going to get a medal for it partly because of the way I had written it up for the paper. The motorman slowed the car with a sudden twirling of the handle of a hand brake shaped like a goose neck to see if I'd come aboard. Riding the complete circuit of the longest trolley line was a favorite pastime whenever you had a spare nickle. I was tempted because it was about the coolest thing you could do on such a day. I waved him on, wondering if he would understand. Probably not. Gus was strictly a baseball man, as we all were, for that matter. Later I heard that after high school he had become a linotype operator and joined the ranks of the itinerant printers of that day who worked from shop to shop across the country. He even worked for a while for the Pensacola *Journal* but that was long after I had begun my own wanderings.

As the trolley clanged and clattered away, the conductor, swinging along the running board, waved to me. His name was Bud Booker and we had a business deal going. In exchange for free copies of the paper and such out-of-town papers as I could pick up around the shop, he would give me free rides all the way around East Hill and back, a journey that consumed more than an hour and took you way out into the woods where there were hardly any houses. This was for pleasure, but it became a money-saving deal whenever Bud was transferred to North Hill, where I lived.

I turned left off Palafox a little way along Intendencia Street to a tiny thoroughfare named De Luna Alley running through to Government Street and the Opera House on the corner of the Plaza Ferdinand, named in the old days for the husband of Columbus' friend, Isabella of Spain. Here the flags of five nations had flown, and they told us in school not to accept the statement that St. Augustine was older than Pensacola.

On the corner across the alley from the newspaper was the Curio Shop of Mrs. Neisius, a widow lady whose son Vincent was the *Journal's* pressman. You could find very interesting things in Mrs. Neisius's shop, like live turtles and snakes and a barrel full of sawdust where alligator eggs would hatch out. You could watch the process if you happened by at the right time. There was also a full-sized stuffed alligator wired to stand on its hind legs at the entrance.

Vince had been trying for months to persuade me to get into the mechanical side of newspapering where I would have a trade, but I was firmly committed upstairs. I knew already what I wanted to do, and I have never done any other work except when forced to by circumstance.

I had, of course, arrived too early, and I realized it when I climbed the dark stairs to the dingy and cluttered editorial room that was connected by a door with the editor's large office across the front of the building, above the business office on the ground floor. I was not exactly sure when the news wire would open on Saturday for the first of two periods. It usually had opened and closed when I arrived after an early supper, and the bulk of the day's news was there to be handled by me and two other somewhat more professional employees, one of whom was the editor himself. On such a small city daily at that time, everybody did everything and anything there was to do from reporting to copy-reading, proof-reading, and make-up, as well as handling whatever pictures there were and writing captions. I still remember one caption, or cutlines, as we called them, from the year before when we printed a big picture of the Titanic after she hit the iceberg. "Titanic in Name and Size, She Ended Her Only Voyage in a Titanic Tragedy". I was very proud of that one and carried it around in my pocket until it was in tatters.

My job was that of a sort of super copy boy, but I had to do a lot of rewriting, which I liked most. They told me, the other two, that, if I wanted to write later on, nothing was better training than doing newspaper rewrite, thereby getting me to do it more eagerly. I always looked forward to these Saturday nights, for I considered this real newspaper work, a cut above collecting small bits of local news here and there about the town. And there was always what seemed to me good newspaper talk to listen to in this room where I would continue to work part-time until I set out one day on a long trail leading through larger shops in larger cities, leading also to the playing fields, especially the golf courses of many lands.

The place was deserted now and very hot. It had been silly to come so early, but something had drawn me to the only place in town where the word would come. There was early activity in back and down below where linotype and press were, but I did not go there. As I sat waiting through the dragging minutes, I tried once more to figure out why this particular golf event should be so vital an occurence to a schoolboy who had never swung a club. It was understandable on no logical grounds. I suppose I was able to "identify" with Ouimet, although that word had not yet come into the teenage vocabulary. Francis was

not yet able to vote and, moreover, he was from the
wrong side of the tracks. Francis was the son of a work-
ingman and lived across the street from the exclusive club
where he had caddied since he was old enough to tote a
bag. He had become a pretty good golfer, too, by imita-
tion, although he had to work at summer jobs all through
his school years. He was good enough to enter the U.S.
Amateur championship that year, but he did not plan to
play in the Open at the club where he had been a caddie
so recently. He was persuaded to send in his entry just to
get the experience. The 1913 Open was expected to be an
exciting one. All the leading American players were in it,
but American golf had an inferiority complex long before
Vardon and Ray, the top two British players, came over in
1913. They were held in awe by all. One of them would,
of course, win the title, and the one who didn't would
finish second.

Everything went about as expected. At the end of playing the regulation seventy-two holes, the two Britishers
were in front, tied at 304. All those who had figured to
press them had faded away. Ouimet had not. Nobody
had paid any attention to him. Nobody outside Massachusetts had heard of him, and anyhow, amateurs were-
n't expected to figure in the Open. On the afternoon of
the final round, the scoreboard showed that Ouimet, still
out on the course, had a chance to catch them. A slim
chance. He would have to play the last six holes in 22
strokes, four pars and two birdies. That was just about
impossible. Inexperienced kids do not do such things under the pressure of the final round of a national championship.

Francis did not know this, so he set out to do it. He got
his first birdie at the 13th and struggled for his pars on the
next three holes. Now he had to save a stroke on one of
the last two holes, which were among the most difficult

on the course. The whole crowd had joined him now, and among them were Vardon and Ray. The tension of this golfing drama had seized them all, and only the boy who had to do it remained calm. Francis measured his 20-foot, downhill-sidehill putt on the 17th green. He stroked it firmly. The ball hit the back of the cup and dropped. As it clicked on the bottom, the staid old club heard a roar from its staid old members and witnessed such joyous antics as have rarely been duplicated. Ten minutes or so later, when the final putt dropped on the 18th green in the late-afternoon shadows of the stately old clubhouse, another terrific outburst took place. The local boy, the ex-caddie, had done it. He had made his par 4 and had tied Vardon and Ray.

Everyone forgot for the moment that the dragons were not yet slain. Francis would have to play off the tie with the great men the next day, Saturday, September 20th.

I had handled the short but exciting wire story of the event the day before, and it had been working as a ferment in me ever since. Caught by the excitement of it, I had taken a few mild liberties to make it even more dramatic than the straightforward story the wire copy told. I couldn't go too far, not knowing anything about golf, but I though I'd added a few nice touches. I had told, I thought movingly, how the local lad from across the street had tied Harry Vardon, the greatest shotmaker in the game's history, and Ted Ray, the longest hitter ever known, at The Country Club, just about the most élite environment imaginable. This was a typically American development, and it was, in a word, tremendous. Now today, Saturday, Ouimet was playing off the tie with the celebrated Britishers, and a small miracle was taking place.

On the Saturday before this one, sports editors of the

nation had looked upon golf as a pleasant recreation of the rich rather than a game whose results were important to many. Now, on this Saturday, front pages were being held up, newspaper publishers as well as sports editors were standing by for a big story to break, and papers around the country were demanding special service out of Brookline. All this, of course, I did not know then, but suddenly, as I sat musing, the phone rang with a clamor that startled me out of my reverie. It was our own small Country Club down along the bayshore. Everyone there wanted to know if there was any news and would I please call when there was. It cheered me to know that I was not alone in my local vigil.

Communications in 1913 were not as rapid or as urgent as they would become with the start of World War I a year later. I did not know how long a round of golf in a championship playoff might be expected to take, nor where exactly Brookline was. It was late afternoon when the telegraph operator, who took the stuff over the wire each day, came up the stairs, his personal telegrapher's key in a little cloth bag he carried in his hand. He was not surprised to see me because of my excitement the day before. I think he was borrowed from either the Western Union or Postal office to take what was called a "pony" or condensed report of the day's top news stories out of the Southern Bureau of the Associated Press in Atlanta. There always were these early and supplementary files on Saturday because the Sunday paper was much larger than the slim affair of weekdays.

I do not remember the operator's name although I saw him daily for many months. Everybody called him Spec, and that may be all I ever did know. He plugged his key into the connection on the table by the window where we all worked, and sat down to wait for the clicks that would tell him that the wire was open. He, too, wanted to know why I was so interested in "this here golf", but I did attempt to tell him.

By now the wait began to seem interminable. Across the alley in a room above the curio shop, someone was playing a grama-phone, its huge morning-glory horn faintly visible behind window curtains moving slowly in the sticky heat. Sousa marches came floating across endlessly. Ever since that day, whenever the name of Ouimet has come up or the 1913 Open at Brookline has been mentioned, there in the background echoing faintly I could hear "The Washington Post March" and "The Stars and Stripes Forever" followed by the monotonous announcement, "Played by the Edison Concert Band . . . Edison Rek-kord".

Spec took off his sweaty shirt, sitting bare from the waist up, and rolled himself another cigarette from the sack of Bull Durham he had placed on the table. He was very deft at it, and I observed carefully because up to then my own efforts had not been very successful. Seeing me watching the operation, he offered to teach me, but I was still a secret user of what our elders called "coffin nails". I decided to pass up an opportunity I felt I could hardly afford to waste, since this ability to roll a proper cigarette carried a certain distinction, and not many adults dared to teach a boy the art in those days. As a matter of fact, I never did learn to roll a proper cigarette. This was the period when smokers were changing over from roll-your-own to "tailor-made" under the influence of a pre-Madison Avenue national advertising campaign, and my real addiction came after experience with such then popular brands as Piedmonts, Home Runs (pack of twenty for a nickel), Picayunes, Sweet Caporals and some fancy things called Egyptian Deities.

At last, almost at evening's fall, the telegraph key began

to click out its jerky cadences. Now there would be news. But it was exasperatingly long in coming. There was a long period of standing behind the operator and watching as he slowly transferred the unintelligible noises to the typewriter page. The day of the visible typewriter had not yet arrived in our shop. On this one, the keys struck upward on the concealed underside of the roller through a ribbon two inches wide, and you had to swing the whole carriage upright to see what had been written.

Spec seemed painfully slow as he tapped out endless unimportant news items. Now and then he stopped altogether to chat with the man at the other end of the wire in the jargon of Morse Code that the old operators employed when gossiping. Spec never went back to work without rolling himself another butt, which he let hang plastered to his lower lip while typing. It seemed impossible to wait any longer when at last he half-turned and said without removing the cigarette, "Here it comes now, Dateline Brookline, Mass." Then, after a few more clicks and a few more taps on the typewriter, "Your boy did it. You better go home now and get something to eat before you have to come back here."

All over the country at this moment, the wires were clicking out the incredible story, a story that would have been rejected immediately if thought up by a fiction writer. But who would dare contrive a hero who had been born across the street from the scene of his triumph, who had learned the game as a caddie on that same course?

Just a few paragraphs came to us down on the Gulf to give us some sense of the excitement and scores. Wholly inadequate, I thought. I felt personally cheated and felt that someone had misjudged the news value of the event. I was right, too. It was much bigger than that. I had been expecting a long, detailed account from Brookline, although I ought to have known better. Now I would have to wait for the New York papers to learn all about it, and that would not be before Wednesday. There was enough detail, though, for me to do a fairly long piece for the paper.

Of course, everyone knows what the news was, because it was the most dramatic story in the long history of golf. Ouimet beat Vardon and Ray by five and six strokes respectively. He was the first amateur to win the U.S. Open. The details can be found in the record books and old newspaper files. What you cannot find there is the effect of the victory, because, tremendous as it was from a competitive point of view, historically it was even more significant. The cheers from Brookline shook the country. Ouimet became a national sports hero, and he made America golf-conscious. In 1913, golf was generally regarded as the exclusive pastime of the wealthy, the aged and the British-born. Now young men everywhere, I among them, began to think about playing the new game. If an ex-caddie, a young man not much older than myself could do this, then golf could not be such an exclusive game. Ouimet's victory popularized the game, took the curse off it, so to speak, and put it on Page One.

It also moved thousands who had hardly considered playing golf before to try the game. It reached farther than that, farther than anyone could know at the time. It reached down to Atlanta and touched an eleven-year-old boy named Bobby Jones, who had also waited that Saturday afternoon for word from Brookline. The wave reached out to Texas to a couple of infants just recently born to the Hogan and Nelson families, and likewise into the Virginia hills to another infant named Samuel Jackson Snead. And it touched the lives of thousands yet unborn, such as Arnold Palmer and Jack Nicklaus. Historians, at odds on many things, are unanimous in declaring that this September Saturday in 1913 was the day when golf first caught the imagination of the American people.

And, finally, it reached into the dingy little office in De Luna Alley where I had waited for the word. Ouimet put golf on the front page of the Pensacola *Journal* all right. I saw to that, and the effect of experiencing it and putting it there after the long period of waiting would last a lifetime. If Francis were alive today, he would be more than eighty years old. He is not only dead, he has entered mythology. At Brookline in 1913, spectator golf in this country was born. That is where the game first began to be a big thing for the modern mercenaries of the multimillion dollar tours.

Little of the future success of golf could have been imagined so far away and so long ago, but, walking home through the silent town after midnight when work was done, I think I must have had a premonition that my journalistic ambition, already set in a certain mold, could be changed. This would not be the last golf story I would handle. I was dreaming the sort of waking dreams that adolescents are forever dreaming.

Reality was the usual nightly stop at the Busy Bees Cafe where Angelo would just be taking the buns and donuts from the oven and would respond as always to a tap on the side door to the kitchen. The bun, all steaming from the oven, was fair exchange for the newspaper hot from the press, and both carried the thrill of things newly born. The smell of bread fresh from the oven has still the power to bring back the approaching dawn of the September day that was a prelude to golfing and newspaper adventures when, just lurching out of boyhood, life was all anticipation, shimmering with the promise of wonderful things, and when time was an invention of the elderly. An age was ending, the innocent period before 1914. An affluent, confident, and, in a way, complacent era in American life was about to turn into the hell of trench warfare, poison gas, and other horrors let loose.

CHAPTER III
Getting to Know Bobby Jones

In the summer of 1919, I was on what the Army called terminal leave. Walking back from the diner through the swaying cars of a train somewhere south of Washington, I picked up part of a newspaper someone had dropped. On the sports page, to which it was folded, I saw that the Southern Open championship was in progress at the East Lake Club in Atlanta and that many of the big names of golf were in it. On the spur of the moment, I decided to stop over in Atlanta the next morning to see the last day of the tournament. This was a sudden decision without thought or consideration, and I can still wonder at it because it led to a meeting with the 17-year-old Bobby Jones, the most important association of my golfing life.

This was the first golf tournament I ever looked at properly, but I had followed golf as closely as possible from afar since 1913 and had acquired a little confused experience in 1916 when the U.S. Open Championship was held at the Minikahda Club, in Minneapolis, where I was working on my third newspaper job, having lasted only a few months on the second in Dallas. I was still not very far above the copy-boy level of journalism and had as yet no connection with sport, but I was now a little closer to the real thing. There was another such lad on the paper, and since, before they started charging admission, all you needed was time and carfare, I persuaded him to go with me to Minikahda.

The player I really wanted to see was Ouimet, but I never found him, not knowing how to go about it in an unfamiliar scene of great confusion. I saw a lot of golfers, but the only one I really remembered was Walter Hagen. He had come on the scene as the successor to Ouimet as the U.S. Open champion in 1914, and for that reason I knew his name well. Hagen finished seventh at Minikahda, but he made a much stronger impression than did Chick Evans, the winner. I had some difficulty recalling

Evans at all, though he won with a record score of 286 that stood for twenty years. Chick also won the U.S. Amateur that summer, the first man to win the two championships in the same year. He kept possession of the two titles for three years because of the war.

It is no doubt unfortunate that, for a golf writer of such long experience, one of the outstanding players in the game's history should remain through the years an obscure, almost shadowy figure, less vivid even than Jerry Travers or Walter Travis, neither of whom I ever saw play and know only from reading and hearing of them. My inability to be moved by Evans has long worried and puzzled me, and it still leaves me with a guilty feeling. Many times I have pondered the question of what it is in some athletes that stirs our sympathy and leaves us with an image, while others of perhaps greater ability and achievement leave us unmoved. It is a theme that runs like a thread through the whole of my sports-writing years and never has been resolved.

What remains from Minikahda was something even less tangible but very real. There I first came a little under the influence, perhaps the spell, of the extraordinary atmosphere of championship golf. There really is nothing like it in sport, and it is the same wherever the U.S. Open and the British Open are played.

The absence of this feeling on that pleasant summer day in 1919 at East Lake struck me at once. I tried to see all the players whose names and deeds I knew, but the only things necessary to record here are that the tournament was won by Long Jim Barnes, who was to be our Open champion in 1921, and that Bobby Jones was second, ahead of all the other well-known professionals. The meeting with Bobby, a seventeen-year-old schoolboy, at the end of the tournament would seem on the surface to have been little more than a casual encounter, so brief and so outwardly routine did it appear. But the first quick impression was so strong that I think that both the school-boy and the older soldier, who was still a youth, felt something special in the meeting. On the train taking me home to Pensacola late that night, I thought long about it. I knew for certain that this was the beginning of something. I knew the inadequacy of words to express what I felt, and I wonder still at all that stemmed from casually picking up that discarded newspaper from the floor of a pullman car. I am wondering if it were not especially for this meeting that I stopped over in Atlanta, and that a result of it was that I later accepted a job with the Associated Press in Atlanta precisely so that I might get to know Bobby Jones.

When I picked up that piece of newspaper and went to East Lake that summer's day, I had no other conscious intent than to get out of uniform and head for New York as quickly as ever I could. I was impatient to get there and find a newspaper job, any kind of job on any newspaper. Now I think there is the possibility that I might never have become a golf reporter at all if I had not gone back to Atlanta and formed this close connection.

Before I returned from the war, Bobby had played in the U.S. Amateur championship at Oakmont and had stirred high excitement in Atlanta and elsewhere by reaching the final, where he was beaten 5 and 4 by Davy Herron, a 20-year-old Oakmont member. Atlanta and the whole country followed Jones's progress with intense interest, for he had already captured the public imagination. It has been forgotten now that the Amateur championship once was almost as big a golfing occasion as the Open itself, or that an amateur was as likely as not to be Open champion in any year. Of the four Opens held just before the First World War interrupted play, amateurs won three—Ouimet in 1913, Jerry Travers in 1915, and Evans in 1916.

In that autumn of 1919, Jones was a precocious undergraduate at Georgia Tech, but he didn't seem entirely comfortable there. I thought he was disturbed by the scientific, technical atmosphere of the Engineering School. Yet he graduated with honors and appeared, to most who knew him, normally happy, and, to some, a carefree college boy. This was an illusion.

When the Amateur Championship of 1920 approached, I had known Bobby for more than a year, becoming progressively closer to and more intimate with him. I was fascinated by his personality—so gentle, so intelligent and so pleasantly charming in an amazingly mature way on a surface that concealed a strong, almost uncontrolled temper. In young Bobby, passionate emotions were a chaotic mixture with first one and then another in control. They were submerged most of the time, but at certain moments they threatened to dominate his personality, his view of himself and the outside world. It was generally believed that Jones during those years was merely going through a protracted period of adolescence. Those close to him knew how much more alarming it was. This gifted young man, perhaps because he was so gifted, had to wrestle with demons.

I sought almost daily contact with him at this time and especially tried to be close whenever possible on the golf course. Once I travelled with friends of his to a tournament in Chattanooga in an old Hudson automobile that got stuck on a long, rain-slick, red clay hill somewhere in North Georgia. I twice had the frightening experience of seeing him come to the very edge of malice in fierce outbursts that neither he nor I understood. I was afraid for him, for I had seen him flushed and shaking in a rage of sudden anger, then drained white a moment later in sudden fear at the nearness of evil. In a sense I shared his deep inner struggle to overcome what, with his intellect, he knew to be ignoble. He knew well that he was poisoning himself with anger, that he must find the inner strength to rise above it. To reconcile this side of his nature with the wonderful young person I knew him to be was a difficult thing for me.

Because of this, I was on the point of throwing up the Atlanta job and going with him to New York for the 1920 championship at the Engineers' Club on Long Island. I was still frightened by what might happen, but I was glad afterward I had not gone. That might have interrupted our relationship too soon, and Bobby himself did not seem to want it. At any rate he was beaten decisively, 6 and 5, in the semi-final by Ouimet, who lost to Evans in the final next day. When Jones returned, I could see at once that he had changed and that something was different. I tried to question him about this and about the Ouimet match. For a while he would say little more than "Francis helped me. You know what I mean." Early in our acquaintance I had questioned him at length about Ouimet, because I was eager to hear everything about Francis, and Bobby was the first peron I had encountered who actually knew him. Most of what I got from him were statements such as "Francis is a fine man" and "There's nobody like Francis".

After the return from Engineers, I began to have a certain faint understanding. I began to see that the young Bobby had for Francis what amounted, if not to actual reverence, then to the greatest possible admiration for him as a human being. I was a long time getting it out of him, and I had to wait much longer to understand that this relationship with an older person of Ouimet's character was the most important thing in the young life of

Bobby Jones. Nearly a lifetime was needed to know how this could be, but understanding began with his remark, "Francis helped me" and with the feeling of vast relief with which it was said.

I think now that it was at that very point, that very day when Jones, with his deep feeling for unspoken thoughts, first realized that his weakness could be his teacher, that he could be strengthened and not enfeebled by the experience through which he was passing. There was an incident in that match with Ouimet at Engineers that infuriated Bob and caused him to lose control, and his admiration for Ouimet made him thoroughly ashamed of such an outburst in the presence of one he revered. "But all Francis really said," Jones told me later, "was 'Let's just play golf, Bobby'". Francis helped him by being Francis in the same way as Bob many years later helped others merely by being Bob. I think that there is little doubt that this exchange on the course with Ouimet that day was the beginning of success in Jones's struggle, the turning point in the "critical match I thought I was losing", as Bob himself expressed it a long time later.

Once he had achieved actual maturity by overcoming this disturbing and dangerous element of his nature, Jones became the most "balanced" person I ever encountered in sport, a man who had achieved a rare harmonious unity of the inner self and outer self which had formerly been at war.

All this lay far ahead and was undreamed of in 1919, a period also made memorable by a red-letter day at the old Ansley Park golf course where I first broke 90, a degree of skill worth mentioning only to confirm my efforts as a serious striver.

CHAPTER IV
The 1923 U.S. Open at Inwood, and the 1926 British Open at Lytham

The year 1923 was a big one for me and for a lot of other people. It was the year in which the new crystal-set radio craze advanced to the point of being taken for granted; a game called Mah Jong was sweeping the country; something called the Younger Generation was on a rampage; the tomb of Tutankhamen was opened in Egypt; the Freudian gospel was putting self-control out of date; millions were singing an idiotic song called "Yes We Have No Bananas"; and the U.S. Open championship came to the Inwood Country Club on the Long Island shores of Jamaica Bay.

The 1923 Open did far more than provide one of the turning points of my life. (I was drawn into the world of big-time golf for the first time as something more than a spectator.) As all golf addicts know, the 1923 Open was the beginning of the reign of Bobby Jones.

I was certain to see and visit with Jones again, and the thought of it gave me pleasure. I would also see Francis Ouimet, and it was now just ten years since Brookline. Francis had done nothing sensational since winning the Amateur in 1914, but he had continued to be "heroic" for me. I had not yet quite completed the process of growing up, but there really is no need to apologize for my still being young in 1923. This was my real introduction to the world of championship golf, and, in spite of some naive misconceptions that led to embarrassing disappointments, it was a good Open at which to begin a golf-writing career.

I had thought I'd walk right in, find Bob Jones, and sit down with him for a pleasant renewal of our friendship. I could hardly have been more mistaken. Jones was seldom around when he was not playing, and at those times he was never alone. Already, without having won a major tournament, he was one of the most popular athletes of the day. Whenever he appeared about the grounds, he was surrounded by people—important people, I thought. My press badge would admit me anywhere, but my role, journalistically speaking, was so miniscule I felt shy about approaching anyone at all. I was nervous and afraid of being challenged by someone in authority, but I did get up the nerve to go into the press tent. I was so obviously bewildered there that one of the Western Union operators accosted me and asked, "You want a wire?" I had to guess what he meant, and I had to say no. My job was to go back to a deserted shop each evening and write a few pages of notes for the next days' early editions, and I had been warned that the stuff would be thrown out when news began to come in from more experienced reporters on the scene, men who didn't even know I was there. The many afternoon papers, competing for newsstand sales, made many editions, and the on-the-spot reporters were kept busy sending something new for each press run. Many of the operators and some of the working reporters in that press tent later became my friends and colleagues, but I did not get very far with it that first week.

My job ought to have been quite easy. The place was swarming with golfers. More than three hundred and fifty had come from all over to try to qualify, and it took four days to reduce their number to the seventy-seven who started in the championship proper on Friday. Even so, I was desperately afraid of falling down on my first golf assignment.

The second day was better. Familiarity with the scene made me less nervous and fearful. I did not yet dare to venture into clubhouse and locker room, where others were getting the sort of stuff I needed, but I felt I might manage it before the week was out. Standing beside the 18th green, I heard someone say that Jones would not play until the afternoon but that Hagen had just started.

So I turned toward the first nine to pick Hagen up. I never got there. The way led past the entrance to the clubhouse, and I saw there a group of about a dozen clustered around Jones. I think I must have been excessively shy in those early days. I knew well that Jones would welcome me, for we had not lost touch, and I thought how fine it would be to join that group in which I recognized Ouimet and Grantland Rice from their pictures. But I could not find the boldness to approach Jones in that company. I stood there and reflected that I would never make a real reporter if I had so little nerve and confidence, but I simply could not make myself do it. I was about to move sadly away when Bob looked up and saw me. Instantly, he called a warm greeting and added, "Come meet Francis Ouimet". We had swapped memories of Brookline, and Bob knew well who was the important one for me. He understood my longing to join them, and his reaction was as natural as the singing of birds.

So at last I shook the hand of the hero of Brookline, and it was revealed to me immediately why this man I had never seen had so caught my affection and that of thousands of others who never had seen him. And why he could help Bobby. It was his goodness. This was a "good" man in the real meaning of full of goodness. He and others in that group took flattering notice of me, and many good things were to spring from this encounter. It mattered greatly to me that these golfing people, especially Ouimet, remembered later that I had been at Inwood.

That incident before the clubhouse steps was the big thing for me on my first assignment—more important even than the climax of the famous Jones-Cruickshank playoff on Sunday—but there were minor encounters I will mention because of their bearing on later events. The big disappointment of the week was Sarazen. From what

I had read, I felt I could have a pleasant chat with one so outgoing as the little defending champion, but I got a rude shock.

It was inexperience that led me to approach him just after he had opened with a 79. Along with this, I didn't know, as I should have, that Gene had come to Inwood still brooding over the humiliation of having failed as the reigning U.S. Open champion to qualify for the British Open at Troon, in Scotland, a little earlier in the year. The golf writers had been rough on him, too, and he was in no mood for a friendly chat when I encountered him waiting to tee off for the second round. I introduced myself and said the usual things. He grunted, turned away, and began to swing his driver in a short arc. I ought to have retreated but thought I'd have another go. I said his 79 was no great handicap for a champion. He then turned on me with so vicious a snarl I thought he might cream me with the club as he shouted for all the world to hear: "What the hell do you newspaper fools know about it? Leave me alone!"

I left him alone. For a long time I left him alone while watching him from a distance. A fascinating little man with a wonderful way of playing golf and one with whom I was finally to form a pleasant and rewarding friendship.

This encounter discouraged me from approaching Hagen, who finished even worse than Sarazen with a closing 86. But how different it was when I did summon the courage to accost Hagen, who was no brooder. He was a most approachable and friendly man, ever ready to lie cheerfully to make a nonentity feel good. I told Walter I had been his guest at Westchester and, without the slightest hesitation, he replied, "Why certainly I remember, son," and stuck out his hand. Hagen made you feel he did remember, and he continued to call me "son" down through the years.

Earlier, on the first day of the championship proper, it was from Francis Powers, a golf writer from the West, that I heard words of wisdom about the way golf clubs were swung and shots made, and we began a lasting friendship. Powers, whom I had met in the group with Jones, let me walk a little way with him in Ouimet's gallery, the first of many such occasions. I don't suppose he realized that he was teaching me golf then and at many later tournaments. On this first occasion, he left me with Ouimet, advising that I take note of Macdonald Smith and Joe Turnesa for beauty of method, while he went to pick up the most beautiful of all, Bob Jones. Since I was under no obligation to follow anyone else, I saw most of the strokes Ouimet made in the first round. Alas, there were 82 of them.

I had a slight feeling of guilt at deserting Ouimet at our very first meeting, so much had he meant to me for ten years, but Jones was working his spell in the tournament. Bob's first victory, after all had seemed lost, naturally had elements of high drama. It was said about the place that, what with the deep frustration Bob had known, if he did not win at Inwood, he would probably give up the chase after titles and go back to playing golf for fun. I knew there was nothing to that. It was not his way. If he dropped out, the cause would not have been failure to win big titles. It would have been failure of another kind, for by now Bob was a mature man, and he had beaten far more formidable opponents than golf courses and golf champions.

Jones won— the first of his thirteen national titles—at the final hole of the 18-hole play-off with a shot that will be remembered after champions who came before and after him are forgotten. Bobby Cruickshank and Jones were tied for the round when they came to the eighteenth; a difficult and frightening hole. It measured 425 yards and its fairway was narrow, with trees and rough running along each side. Then there was a lagoon that cut across in front of the green. Cruickshank drove first and hooked into a part of the rough from which he would very likely have to lay up short of the lagoon. Jones pushed his drive a little and it ended up in the edge of the rough along the right. That much I saw from behind the tee, and then I let the crowd in its sudden surge for position shut me out completely. They were ten deep behind Jones's ball and they stretched in a long curve across the fairway. I thought both players would take 5s, and I was wondering if they would go on into extra-holes or play another round the next day when Cruickshank played his ball safely short of the lagoon. I took it for granted that Jones would do the same, and so I did not try to get closer. Probably everybody else there knew he was going for the green and that, if he made it, he would finally be champion. I could hear the click of club on ball, and I thought I caught a glimpse of the ball in the air, but I wonder if I really did. I did not know that it had made the green until the great roar made it unmistakeable what had happened.

Each time I have visited Inwood in later years, and they have been many, I could close my eyes and see the whole picture again whenever I walked up the eighteenth fairway.

The events at both Muirfield and St. Andrews in the summer of 1926 were dramatic and they had a direct bearing on the British Open at Lytham, the career of Bob Jones, and especially on the Grand Slam. Bob said that the thought of a possible Slam first came to him that summer, even though he was unsuccessful in the first and the last of the four major championships that year. He was beaten in the sixth round of the British Amateur by a Scottish youngster named Andrew Jamieson after having played the most devastating golf to that point. It was this defeat, Bob said, that made him decide to play in the British Open two weeks later. He also revealed, though not until many years later, that he played that losing match with a severe "crick" in his neck that restricted his swing and gave him much pain.

Bob never spoke of that to me until his return to Britain the following year. He said he knew I wouldn't mention it in the paper, but he didn't want me to think he would offer an excuse for a defeat. If Jones had won that match with Jamieson and gone on to win the title, one may speculate that there might never have been a Grand Slam. Well, he stayed over in 1926, won the British Open at Lytham and then the U.S. Open at Scioto barely two weeks later. He was beaten in the final match of the U.S. Amateur, 2 and 1, by George Von Elm. Since Jones felt he could have won the British Amateur, did win the two Opens, and was narrowly beaten in the last match of the U.S. Amateur, the idea that a man could win all four in the same year became firmly implanted in his mind.

Because the 1926 British Open was such an adventure for me and was Bob Jones's first victory in Great Britain, I am inclined to write of it at too great length. The details are more vivid in my mind than those of tournaments played only a few years ago, and I feel the urge to recall every little thing and set it down again. This would not be appropriate. The whole tournament really came down to a couple of shots, one justly celebrated because it won the title, the other legendary although it did not come off.

Lytham, a famous golfing ground which has been on the regular rotation of the British Open's seaside venues since the year of Jones's victory, had always produced a worthy champion—Jones in 1926, Bobby Locke in 1952, Peter Thomson in 1955, Bob Charles in 1963, Tony Jacklin in 1969—and it has not changed very much. It lies in the

village of St. Anne's-by-the-Sea, and the rail line on which
I arrived from Liverpool runs right past most of the holes
of the first nine through a narrow passage lined on the
other side by a long row of attached brick houses, with
only a low wooden fence alongside the course. My first
impression was of terrain flat and largely treeless, no
great severity, and a certain vague artificiality. I had pic-
tured Lytham as a seaside course, but the Irish Sea was
out of sight a mile or so beyond the houses of the town.
There were plenty of man-made sandhills and bunkers,
and the second nine turned inland away from puffing
trains and other disturbances. Lytham, I heard someone
say just before I set out to inspect it, was a course on
which only a complete golfer could win, and the man who
could control the middle irons would have an advantage.
Jones was very good with those clubs, and it was, in fact,
a shot with a middle iron that made the difference. He
won with 72-72-73-74. That does not sound like much
today when scores are forever in the 60s and players who
have never won a tournament are below par week after
week. But it was as low a score as ever had been made in
the British Open. People forget that spectators once got a
kick out of such scoring. In every golfing age we thrill to
the record score, whatever it is. At that time we hailed a
71 because it was one less than 72, just as in the 1970s we
think 64 wonderful because it is one less than 65.

There were a lot of fine players in this field, including
Jim Barnes, the defending champion, and I planned to see
all of them. But really, the only ones that matter for this
account are Jones, Hagen, and Al Watrous, a young
American professional. Hagen, who had won the Open
twice and would win it twice again, led on the first day
with a glittering round of 68, only part of which I saw, but
Jones and Bill Mehlhorn were in front after two rounds,
tied at 144.

For the final two rounds on Friday, Jones was paired

with Watrous, who trailed by two strokes. I went more than halfway with them in the morning, then doubled back to pick up Hagen, who had started more than an hour later. I was at the 18th, though, when Jones and Watrous finished their round, and I had a sinking feeling when I saw that Bob's two-stroke lead had become a two-stroke deficit. Watrous had done a 69 to Bob's 73.

In the final round, it was first Jones chasing Watrous, then Hagen chasing Jones, and the outcome depended on two shots that have long since been regarded as historic golf occasions. Since Hagen was so far behind Jones and Watrous, I went all the way with the other two. Jones gave me fits. He was not playing the sort of golf that was needed to close the gap, but he finally did get even at the 16th after struggling for many of his pars. Then he promptly pulled his tee shot at the 17th into serious trouble to set the stage for the climax. The 17th measured a few yards more than 400, and the fairway bent a little to the left around a large, rolling sweep of sand. Jones's ball lay clean on the sand, but between it and the green were a nearby bunker and a series of dunes. He was a long way from the green, probably 180 yards, and could not see the flag. Neither could I from where I stood, and I did not move. I wanted to see the shot itself, and I was almost afraid to look.

Watrous had hit a good straight drive, and, playing first, he put his ball on the green. Jones walked straight across the fairway from left to right and stood there looking first at the green, then at the spot where he had put his tee shot. I wondered what he was thinking, looking first one way and then back, and I have wondered a thousand times since what it is that tournament players think about when they stand there putting off the moment for taking action. Not that Jones dawdled. Far from it. He always decided quickly, then went to work.

Now he looked, came back with his mind already made

up, and what I remember more acutely than the shot itself
was how drawn and almost ill Bob's face appeared as he
stepped into the sand and settled his feet. Then he struck
the ball with a mashie iron, about a No. 4 by later grad-
ings. A big shout far down the fairway told us that the ball
had safely reached the green. When Watrous eventually
took three putts, Jones moved a stroke ahead. He picked
up another stroke at the last hole and so won by two,
having played the last five holes in par figures. Par was
very good golf on that course that day.

Jones's second to the 17th will always be remembered
because it has been properly commemorated by a plaque
placed on the spot from which it was played, and the
mashie iron which Jones used now hangs in the Lytham
clubhouse, properly identified. What made it one of the
finest shots ever brought off in championship play? The
ball lay on dry sand. A fraction too much sand, and the
ball might move hardly at all and end up in a worse place.
A fraction too little sand or none at all, and the ball might
skitter and run into some really horrid spot. With the
target out of sight, the stroke also had to be judged exactly
so that the ball would become airborne instantly, carry
175 yards or more, and stop quickly after reaching the
green. It was only after I had heard the shot discussed
that I came to have some understanding of its difficulty
and the boldness, technical mastery and even artistry involved in bringing it off. Even so, I had now been present
when Bob Jones, the greatest of them all, had won his first
U.S. Open at Inwood and his first British Open at Lytham
with two shots that still glow brightly in the memories of
all who saw them.

The other famous shot at Lytham, I think, might well
have been forgotten by all of us if it had not been kept
alive by much retelling and dramatic rewriting. I am not at
all sure that it was not actually born in the retelling. It was

struck by Hagen long after Jones had finished and been congratulated. Hagen had a chance to catch Bob certainly. And there were reports that he was doing extraordinary things late in the afternoon. He was some holes back. I believed these reports. You could never be sure about Hagen, however slim the chance. That's what everyone said. It was a good idea to keep an eye on him, and a lot of us did.

However, when we came up the 18th fairway with him after his fine drive, we all knew his chance was gone. It was a straight hole a little under 400 yards with the green almost under the clubhouse balcony. Walter's drive from the 72nd tee had been his 290th stroke, so that he could gain a tie now only by holing his next shot from about 150 yards out. Hagen's flair for the spectacular was so well known that some persons in the gallery may actually have thought that he might do it. It was not impossible. People had made holes-in-one from greater distances.

The story told afterward was that Hagen made a production of walking up to the green to make sure the flag was attended and that the attender should be alert and ready to yank the stick out to let the ball fall into the cup. Hagen, it is related, made gestures and said words that conveyed clearly to the crowd that the great Sir Walter never played for second place. He was going for a first-place tie and a shot at victory in a play-off. And, the story goes, he played the shot only after making sure of the proper tension and suspense, and then came so close to holing it as to take your breath away.

This is a wonderful story and has become part of the game's fact and tradition. I am sorry to relate that I do not remember it that way, and this time I feel sure I am right. I stood in the gallery behind Hagen and what I remember is that the ball went all the way through the green, passing not really very close to the cup and winding up in a

bunker—some said in a flower-bed near the clubhouse—
and that Hagen took three more strokes to get down,
ending up with 295 and in a tie for third place.

I believe now that the whole thing was built on little
that actually happened. Golfers often walked toward the
green before making long approach shots, and thousands
of approach shots that passed near the hole have wound
up in bunkers. Hagen had long finished his competitive
career and become one of the game's revered figures before I ever got around to bringing this matter up with him.
I was on the point of speaking several times but something stopped me. I think I wanted it to be true. When I
finally did question him, he laughed and said something
like the following:

"Don't you remember, son? I never deny any story
about myself. I don't go around breaking down my image
at this late time in my life."

Walter was right, of course. One scuttles golf legends at
one's peril.

It has been said of Hagen countless times that he never
played for second, and it was true. But I am wondering as
I write what would have been his attitude if he had been
there in the 1970s when second place often was worth
$15,000 to $25,000, and sometimes more. People who finish second these days soon become millionaires if they do
it often enough.

CHAPTER V
The Haig Wins His Last Major

I did not get back to Scotland for more than two years, but I had a wonderful dose of it in 1929 and for ten years afterwards. In 1928 the British Open was held at Royal St. George's, Sandwich, on the Kentish coast and on a sea-side course that some thought the most charming of all. Among these was Walter Hagen, who won his third British title there that year.

I had a guilty feeling about this championship because the occasion was more memorable for the opportunity to renew acquaintance with Gene Sarazen, who finished second, than for Hagen's victory. I should say that I made the acquaintance of Sarazen, since he appeared to have no recollection of ever having seen me before. I approached him still with some misgiving and was relieved when he did not remember. This time we got along very well.

Hagen's victory, in fact, was not as exciting as Sarazen's failure, a mishap of which he had told charmingly with the help of Herbert Warren Wind in "Thirty Years of Championship Golf", one of the very best reminiscence books any champion has produced. The memory of this week of association with Sarazen and his picturesque caddie, Skip Daniels, is especially pleasant because of the unfortunate fact that I never was present at one of the Squire's big moments, even though he had more of them than most champions. I was not there when he took the British Open at Prince's in 1932, because the Great Depression was on and newspapers were cutting corners and salaries. For the same reason, I did not make Fresh Meadow a few weeks later to see that wonderful outburst of scoring, twenty-eight holes in 100 strokes, that swept Sarazen to victory in the 1932 U.S. Open.

I stuck with Gene for most of the time at Sandwich in 1928, and over the years, I think, I may have seen him play more golf than any other of the great champions. There was something carefree and joyous about his game that gave me more pleasure over the long run than almost any other golfer except Jones. When I encountered Gene at Sandwich, he was a friendly little man with an infectious grin nearly always on his round dark face. He had a method of striking the ball that fascinated me. I loved to see him swing a club and couldn't get enough of it. He seemed almost casual in spite of his serious, no-foolishness way of playing. Quite a number of fine players of his generation who came from the caddie yard, an institution that has disappeared, also had something of this attitude.

Sarazen played the big tournaments year after year right into the late fifties, his own and the century's, and you could be sure he would give you full value with a round or two of fine golf full of joyful shots. He is now, I am told, scoring his age at 76. A great and classic shot-maker, the Squire always looked over the crowd to see which of his friends were following him. No matter the tournament situation, no matter where on the course you picked him up, Gene soon knew you were there. He took it as his due, and we, his old friends, took it as a duty and a privilege. In the days of multi-million-dollar tours, the Squire was our bridge to the more pleasant and perhaps greater days of his own youth and ours.

On reflection, I do not find it strange that, because of Sarazen, I remember so little of the other play at Sandwich, even though Hagen in his later years often referred to his victory in the 1928 British Open as his greatest thrill. He felt that way, I think, due to two things: the British public at last reacted wonderfully and warmly to him; and it was here that Hagen first met the Prince of Wales, later King Edward VIII and still later the Duke of Windsor. This was the beginning of that rather charming and, one might say, morganatic friendship that endured as long as Hagen played international golf. Some of us exaggerated a little in writing of this relationship, but it was a real one, and the story is perfectly true that once during a friendly four-some, Hagen, in the hearing of those standing by, said to the Prince, "Hold the flag, Eddie".

Hagen's victory at Sandwich—75-73-72-72—292, two strokes lower than Sarazen—was hailed in the British press as a marvelous performance, but a little later on I could remember more of Sarazen's golf in losing than of Walter's in winning. That made me feel guilty and a little ashamed, but after I had seen and written of Hagen's fourth victory the following year at Muirfield, I no longer felt remiss. That Open I remember best of all the golf I saw Hagen play, and I think it can be cited as an achievement that proclaimed him one of the most skillful golfers the game has known.

It is appropriate to say here, I think, that all of us who wrote golf in Hagen's day made too much of his flamboyant showmanship, his gamesmanship, his spectacular and captivating egoism, and his extraordinary confidence. We did not make nearly enough of his golf. Undoubtedly, he was one of the most colorful figures sport has known, and he certainly was good company when work was done. But he was much more than just a showman in the ordinary sense. He was a "presence" in the same sense that a great artist of the stage or a great musician is a presence. A communication between artist and audience takes place even before he begins to perform. So it did with Hagen. His mere arrival on the scene did something, caused something to happen. His every appearance seemed to be accompanied by the figurative blaring of trumpets and a metaphorical waving of banners, and Walter was perfectly conscious at all times of his role as performer.

You were always, it seemed, writing about Walter's exploits rather than the quality of his play, and the truth is that his personality and character were such that you could hardly avoid doing so. He was one hell of a golfer, and I doubt if any player excelled him from a purely technical point of view. The purists faulted him, but the purists want beauty along with perfection, and when that blessed combination occurs in a Jones or a Snead, it is certainly a wonderful thing to see. Hagen was not that pretty a golfer. They said his stance was too wide, that he swayed when he hit the ball and didn't drive very straight. Let us forget this nonsense. Let us remember instead the remarkable shots he hit and also keep in mind the one thing that separated him from nearly all his contemporaries, champions and near champions. This was the clearly obvious fact that Walter knew beforehand that he was going to hit those stupendous shots. While others still were unsure at the top of the backswing if they really could bring off a critical stroke at a critical moment, Walter knew with certainty before he started the club back that he would play it superbly. Self-doubt never entered his mind for an instant. That was why Hagen was such a fearsome match-player, carrying off four straight PGA titles at match play from 1924 to 1927 and five in all. That is also why his gamesmanship was so effective. Nothing seemed beyond him.

Muirfield was to be Hagen's last championship victory. For me, it was the zenith of his career. He came to it directly from what would have been for most people a humiliating defeat, a 10-and-8 loss to George Duncan in the Ryder Cup matches. It was getting to be a pattern. The year before he had taken a whopping 18-and-17 pasting from Archie Compston the week before winning the Open at Sandwich. The British used to shift the dates of the Open from one year to the next in those days, and in 1929 they moved it up to May 6–8, the earliest I can remember. Probably it was because the PGA had scheduled the first Ryder Cup series to be played in England for April 26–27.

The American assault in the Open that year amounted almost to an invasion. Besides the ten members of the Ryder Cup team, a group of British-born American players went over, and, in all, more than twenty of our leading players came to Muirfield for the qualifying rounds. The British Open still was rated the No. 1 tournament in the world. Beginning in 1921, golfers from across the Atlantic had won the British Open seven of the previous eight years. They were to win it five more times before the American dominance was ended by Henry Cotton in 1934.

When the American Ryder Cup team had arrived at Moortown, near Leeds, for the 1929 match, the players had been just a little cocky because of their strength on paper—Hagen, Sarazen, Leo Diegel, Horton Smith, Joe Turnesa, Al Watrous, Johnny Farrell, Ed Dudley, Johnny Golden, and Al Espinosa. Following the shock of their defeat by the British, in which Turnesa, Watrous, Sarazen, Hagen, and Farrell all were beaten in the singles, they came to Muirfield in a more subdued mood. All but Hagen. When I looked up Walter on the day before the qualifying began, I wanted to discuss with him the Ryder Cup defeat so that I could write what was called a "mailer", a feature piece sent by mail to save cable tolls. Hagen would have none of that. I don't recall his exact words, but this is what he said: "Forget Moortown, son. It's a dirty word. This is Muirfield. I'm pretty sure I can win here. Go look at the course and the weather. I've been here nearly a week and I'm ready." This from the man who had just taken a bad personal beating and captained a losing team. It really is astonishing when I look back on the effect Hagen could have on a listener. He seemed to know he was going to win at Muirfield, and I felt almost that I shouldn't be thinking he might not. Such confidence in an athlete I have never encountered elsewhere. This also was the effect Hagen often had on opponents, to whom, the story goes, he would say at the start of a tournament, "Well boys, who's going to be second?"

Muirfield is almost in Edinburgh's front yard, a dozen miles out along the South coast where the Firth of Forth empties into the North Sea. It is the gem of a cluster of some of the finest seaside golf courses in the world. It is the home of the Honourable Company of Edinburgh Golfers, the oldest golf club in existence, and the course, unlike the other stalwart Scottish links on the Open rotation, is the property of a private club. Very private. It became well-known to American golfers in more recent years, but in 1929 Muirfield was just another Scottish seaside links on which they played the British Open from time to time. The whole course lies open to the fierce winds that blow off the water. There are no trees to protect it other than a copse of stunted growth called Archerfield Wood. It is exceptional golfing ground with many striking sand hills and views of the sea that makes it seem a part of the course.

The holes at Muirfield were so arranged that the wind blew from every point of the compass during a round. The first nine ran in a rough clockwise circle, with the ninth green near the clubhouse. The second nine described a counter-clockwise circle inside the first. It was not a course where the dunes figured as prominently in the play as they did at other seaside links, but it had fierce stretches of rough in 1929. The narrow fairways were well outlined by it, and the greens were surrounded by sinister bunkers. These bunkers, and most of the others among the two hundred scattered about the course, were large and deep and had walls made of turf bricks to keep the sand from blowing away.

Conditions were not good that week. Except for one day, the second of the tournament proper, the weather was the worst I ever encountered in golf. It was simply cruel, cold enough on the qualifying days and the first day of play to harden the ground and cause ice crystals to form wherever moisture collected. Plenty of moisture did collect from drenching rain squalls blown in off the water by gale-force winds. And then, after one blessed day of glorious sunshine and breeze, all-day winds blew in off the water at forty to fifty miles per hour on Friday when the final two rounds were played. Both the scores and the clothing worn by the players reflected the weather. Most of the qualifiers wore heavy underwear and outer clothing; some even wore overcoats, scarves and mittens while walking between shots. Hagen, having no longjohns, wore two pair of pajamas with newspaper stuffed inside them, an insulating arrangement he permitted me to examine. The other American players also bundled up with whatever they had, but the only one of them I remember is the slender, elegant, but shivering Johnny Farrell, one of the pleasantest acquaintances of a lifetime in golf, whom I encountered here for the first time. Johnny was the reigning U.S. Open champion and the most recent member of the most exclusive organization in golf, the I-Beat-Bob-Jones Club. He had joined it by winning the play-off in the U.S. Open at Olympia Fields the previous June.

The first-round scores were not bad under the conditions. The rain came in intermittent squalls, the wind was high, the skies were angry and menacing, and the prospect was bleak. Hagen had a 75 which, though it left him well back, he considered good enough. And then on the second day when the wind dropped, miraculously, it seemed, after the three days we had endured, Walter played a truly awesome 67, a record both for course and tournament. I saw a lot of this round, for I was on the course the whole day. It was exhilarating. The air had wine in it, the water was full of white caps and white sails, and the larks were actually singing. I had read many Scottish golf reports that included singing larks, but this was the only time they ever sang for me.

One of the pleasures of golf at that time was watching Macdonald Smith, and a bonus for going with him on this day was that he was partnered by Harry Vardon, who may have been the finest golfer of all time. Vardon, at fifty-nine, looked old and positively ill, but something of his elegant style still lingered. It was good to see him, and especially in the company of Mac Smith, whose shotmaking was so splendid that even the uninitiated enjoyed it. As I try to clarify my impressions of Vardon, there comes back to me an anecdote related by some golf enthusiast walking beside me that day. He was an Englishman, but I don't remember him clearly. In any event, he said that when Vardon was asked to join the Temperance Movement, he replied, "Moderation is essential in all things, Madam, but never in my life have I failed to best a teetotaler".

I had come with Vardon and Smith to the ninth. Waiting there, I walked over to the eighteenth green. Hagen was playing his second. His approach hit the flag and dropped next to the hole for a sure birdie. Much was made of this shot in the papers, but Walter called out, "Luckiest shot I ever hit". Later he said he might have needed three more strokes to get down if the ball hadn't tangled with the flag.

Hagen's 142 for the first thirty-six holes, placed him two strokes behind Diegel's leading 140 and two in front of

Abe Mitchell's 144, with Percy Alliss at 145. Nearly everyone had improved his score in the improved conditions,
and, with two rounds to play on the final day, four or five
other Americans were in reach of the leader.

The East Coast of Scotland has produced some prodi-
gious storms, but I doubt if any Open ever was concluded
in such terrible weather. The blow which earlier had
seemed a gale now seemed a hurricane. It howled and
screamed and sent huge combers rolling onto the
beaches. It seemed to come from all directions, and if you
did not brace your feet, you could be blown off them.
Early starters taking their stance on the tee lost their bal-
ance and had to try again. Balls were tossed every which
way, and it was a lucky man who did not find a well-hit
drive winding up among the terrible whins and heather.
There was no rain now, and the ground had become hard
with lots of run. Hagen was due off in mid-morning, and
I could hardly believe it when I saw him coming in off the
course a bit before his starting time. He had actually been
out in that gale for an hour or more to watch the early
starters battle the wind. He winked at me as he passed
and said he'd be back soon.

So this was the happy-go-lucky Hagen, the Sir Walter of
world-wide playboy reputation who never worried. This
was, in fact, a very serious Hagen. Bob Harlow, his often
harrassed manager, had no trouble with a dilatory charge
here. Hagen was even more confident now than usual,
and he seemed fit. It was odd that this high-liver, this
keeper of late hours, should seem to be in better shape to
tackle the terrible conditions than the younger, more careful livers who went to bed early. They moved nervously
and apprehensively into the gale that morning. Hagen
went with the old supreme confidence of his that bor-
dered on arrogance. Actually, Hagen had been getting up
early all week. I think he wanted this one badly and sus-
pected it might be his last.

"You coming with the winner?" he said in some surprise at seeing me still there when he returned to the first
tee. "I figure about 150 will do it today. What do you
think?" I wasn't thinking, just marvelling.

I didn't go all the way with him, but I wished afterwards that I had seen every stroke. I had neither the clothing for it nor the fortitude, but I could have learned a lot.
I went only far enough at first to see what Hagen was up
to. He was playing on each hole—even on some of the par
3s—a low ball that ran on the cold hard ground but ran
only as far as he intended it should. And he was using an
iron with the flattest face possible for nearly every long
shot. He hardly ever let the ball get above what used to be
called quail-high, and thus he overcame the blustery wind
that others could not handle. He deliberately played some
approaches a little short of the green, placing his trust in
his ability to get down in two from anywhere near the
green. Walter knew wherein lay his strength. He knew
that on and around these greens he was the best in the
field, and this knowledge gave him his arrant confidence.
He knew he was strong where his rivals were weak.

Some of those in contention managed to control their
full shots fairly well in the wind. Others chipped and
putted well. Only Hagen combined the two all day long.
He missed an approach or a putt here and there, but he
got his 75 that morning, and at 217 for three rounds he
was leading by four strokes when he came in for lunch.
Diegel had taken an 82 for 222 and Alliss a 76 for 221.
When Walter set out in early afternoon, he was even more
confident because, as he said, conditions had grown
worse and only he could hold what he had. The wind
actually had risen and become more blustery and harder
to gauge. And it was cold. Oh, it was cold all right.

"Where were you?" Walter asked during his break for
lunch, referring to the second nine of the morning round.
"It was lots of fun out there." He continued approxi-

mately as follows: "Go on back inside now. It's getting worse. I won't need another 75, but I'll go for it anyhow."

He got it after a 35 for the first nine, even with a 6 at the ninth, and won by six strokes with 292. Mitchell and Alliss were at 300, but Americans had taken seven of the first ten places.

If I have given the impression that Hagen played that miserable day without a gallery, that is wrong. Even in that weather, a surprisingly large number of Scots went with him, and they knew well what they were seeing. As always, they stimulated Hagen to a noble response. I recall individual shots vaguely if at all, but two I do remember and I still can see them. The first came at the 13th, a par-3 to a high, dangerously narrow green that had a big mound on the left. Walter hit his tee-shot deliberately into the mound, and his ball rolled down onto the green and gave him a putt for a birdie. I do not remember on which hole the other marvelous shot occurred. I only know that Walter was in one of those deep greenside bunkers, the ball up close to the perpendicular, sodded front wall. A blasting shot was clearly indicated, but Hagen nipped the ball as cleanly as if he had picked it up in his fingers and dropped it at the hole. Here we saw the real quality of Walter Hagen as technician and competitor. Though this was his last victory in a major championship, it was not the end of him. He continued to be a prominent tournament player for another ten years, and we were to have a final golfing adventure together in Scotland not long before World War II.

CHAPTER VI
The Greatest Women's Match
Ever Played

The British Ladies' championship was held at St. Andrews the week after the Open that summer of 1929, and it held special interest for both American and British correspondents. Glenna Collett, who had won three U.S. Women's titles and would win three more, had come over to make another bid for the British. That was reason enough to be on hand, but it was only half of it. Joyce Wethered, called by nearly everyone the greatest female golfer ever, had come out of retirement, the British papers said, "to repel the American invasion". There was a lot of feeling in England about British titles going overseas, but the British Ladies' title had never been won by an American girl, and they wanted to keep it that way.

They had feared for the worst, however, when Miss Wethered had retired. She had beaten Miss Collett at Troon in 1925 in her last tournament, so the popular press made quite a stir over Miss Wethered's "patriotic gesture". She herself said it was just that she had always wanted to win at St. Andrews, and the championship had not been played on the Old Course since she was a child. It made a good story, though, and we all went along with it.

I was reluctant to leave Edinburgh unexplored so soon after Muirfield. Brief glimpses had been fascinating. Edinburgh is one of the most majestic cities in all Europe, still very much the capital of a kingdom that has not existed for two centuries. Here the pulse of an older Scotland seems still to beat. More than two hundred years of a common language, the same currency, and the same history have not made the two people the same. The Scots gave golf to the English but retained their Scottishness.

Walking the Royal Mile from Edinburgh Castle high above the town to Holyrood, it needs little imagination to call up the tragic Mary Stuart, who played golf, and to feel the flow of Scottish history. And besides, those other famous courses along the East Lothian coast demanded attention: Dalmahoy, with its three-storied Georgian clubhouse, and the Royal Burgess Golfing Society of Edinburgh, founded in 1735. This pleasant duty had to wait, and late on the day after Muirfield, I followed my British colleagues north of the Firth of Forth and on to the marvelous old town of St. Andrews and to what seems to me now one of the pleasantest weeks in a long string of British summers filled with storm and sunshine. This was the first visit on which I had time to loaf, and I wandered about the town in the long Scottish twilight when work was done and in the early mornings before it began, getting acquainted with a surprising number of townspeople. I think I must have fallen under the spell of St. Andrews as so many other visitors have.

The Old Course was full of people when I arrived on the Saturday before the Tuesday when the tournament was to begin. They mingled freely with the entrants in the Ladies' Championship who were taking their final warm-up. I did so too, and had a long leisurely Sunday to look over the celebrated course. I had seen it and walked it before, but I could not say I knew it until that tournament. As is well-known to golfers, the Old Course, one of four courses wedged into the thumb of land between St. Andrews Bay and the Eden River, is a public course on which anyone may play for a small fee. Members of the local golf clubs also play it. The principal club is the Royal and Ancient whose clubhouse stands like a fortress, or a railroad station, behind the first tee.

It was in 1834 that King William IV was prevailed upon to become the patron of the golf club in St. Andrews, the second club to be formed in Scotland and already the respected leader in guiding the growth of the game. William IV agreed to become the club's patron, and it could henceforth call itself The Royal and Ancient Golf

Club of St. Andrews. I was not admitted to this royal,
sandstone clubhouse on this occasion, since the R. & A.
had not yet recognized the right of the press to occupy the
clubhouse. I did not pass the threshold for some years,
but, in this respect, I was well ahead of every British Open
champion except Harold Hilton and Bob Jones. Professionals still were required to remain outside. When the
sanctuary finally had been opened to us, Henry Longhurst, that delightful and perceptive correspondent of the
London *Sunday Times,* declared under oath that the first
words he heard after crossing the threshold into the "Big
Room" came from an old gentleman seated before the
fire, who said, "I must agree, Sir, that a certain lack of
discipline is to be observed among the younger generation today."

It also is well-known that many people love the Old
Course and some do not, but most of those who do not
generally come to do so if they study it and play it long
enough. Some excellent golfers have testified to a deep
disappointment on their first visit. Other have indulged in
ecstacies without knowing the place at all, and some have
called it great because they were reluctant to say otherwise. The course is all it is said to be. While it appears to
have been laid out casually centuries ago, it still is a fine
test today, although players now use a ball that travels a
hundred yards farther from every tee. My own first impression of the Old Course was that no architect in his
right mind would think of laying it out the same way if he
were starting from scratch.

Golf reporters in my early days saw comparatively little
play by women. There always seemed to be something
else going on that needed to be covered, and the events
women played were considered inconsequential from an
editor's point of view. There was no women's profes-

sional golf at all, and only the local, district and sectional tournaments were regularly reported by the papers. I had never covered a women's national event and had seen few of the best girls in any kind of tournament play. I had observed Miss Wethered on a few non-championship occasions, which had been her only appearances since 1925, and once I saw her in a mixed-foursome competition with her brother Roger as her partner. Like everyone else, I had been impressed with her style, but I did not suppose she would be good enough to beat Glenna again after four years away from tournament golf. This now seems a bit strange since I had not seen Glenna at all, and I knew very well that Bob Jones looked upon Joyce as practically an equal. I accepted Glenna on faith, and I realized that her record was the finest compiled by any lady golfer who had risen to the top in our country. I felt certain that Glenna would win, although she had returned empty-handed from her other journeys to Britain.

The meeting of these two young women was built into a terrific international confrontation comparable to the meeting of Suzanne Lenglen and Helen Wills on the tennis court at Cannes a few years earlier, and the press corps on hand was comparably large. When their names appeared on opposite sides of the championship draw, it was taken for granted that they would meet in the final, a development much less certain in golf than in tennis. Happily it came about, and that Saturday remains the most memorable day of women's golf for me.

I did not see as much of Miss Wethered's play through the early rounds as I should have, because I was trying to see every stroke Glenna played. Besides being rather taken with Glenna, it was she about whom I would write each day, and there was no other way to learn about a match than to follow it, noting the key strokes and the holes won and lost. You had to hustle if you wanted to know these things before writing, and those who write the best golf still hustle.

I saw a good deal of the two girls off the course. In St. Andrews you were bound to see them since everybody went to the same places. Glenna was stopping at the Grand Hotel, where I also had a room, and she and Joyce seemed to be very friendly. They were together a lot, two very attractive young women, and the two best golfers of their sex in all the world. Both were perfectly natural, friendly and charming, but I made no effort to impress myself on either because I believed then that athletes were entitled not to be bothered unduly by morning-paper reporters. There were always plenty of afternoon-paper reporters, tabloid and wire-service men who really needed to speak with them. They did not lack attention, and they both went through it with a good deal of dignity considering that everything was overdone in the Fabulous Twenties.

So, having got the two of them safely through to the final, we all were set for two rounds over the famous course that Saturday in May with high hopes of a good story to write for the Sunday paper. I was confident it would be about an American victory. That was because Glenna's last two victories on Friday over eighteen holes had been most impressive. She had come to the big test with her best game well in hand.

I wonder still if any girl anywhere in the world ever played finer golf than Glenna did at the start of their match. For eleven holes she did not make a single mistake. The hole-by-hole notes I made had that piece of information written opposite the figure 12 on the card. I made this note as they were standing on the 12th tee with the River Eden at their backs. This is where the course, having made the celebrated "loop"—the seventh through the eleventh—turns back, and the golfers now play to the pins on the right-hand side of the double greens as they head back to town. Glenna was now three under level 4s and five up. These figures represent terrific golf on such a course, and I was thinking it would not be such an exciting story to write if this kept up. What strange thoughts we entertain during a long match, when there is plenty of time to play with them! The 12th is a short par-4 whose green is shared with the sixth hole. Both girls avoided the trouble on it and were comfortably on the green with their seconds. Glenna, putting first, left her ball close to the cup. She had left herself little more than two or three feet for her par.

Miss Wethered said afterward that the 12th was "the crux of the whole game". She thought that if Glenna had not missed that three-foot putt, which would have won the hole and made her six up—Joyce herself had been guilty of "criminally taking three putts"—the results never would have been in doubt. I do not know about that, but I still can feel the shock of Glenna missing her putt for her par. I had noted it as being shorter than three feet, and it certainly wasn't a difficult putt. Thinking it was a sure thing, I was moving away from the green to be in position to watch the drives from the 13th tee. I saw the miss over my shoulder. I stopped still, and I must have exclaimed, too, as the crowd let out the kind of noise that always accompanies unexpected failure—half gasp, half shout—quickly followed by a wild scramble to get to the next vantage point.

I thought, "Good Heavens! How could Glenna have been so careless!" Then I had a first faint glimmer of foreboding. I had seen Miss Wethered react quickly and punish mistakes, especially in defeating Molly Gourlay, one of the best players in Britain, a couple of rounds earlier. Nothing was lost, though. Glenna had got a half, and that one little mistake in twelve holes indicated how well she was playing. If she could go in to lunch five up, that should insure victory in the afternoon.

As I walked slowly with the uncontrolled crowd swirling past me toward the 13th tee, I realized with something of a shock how badly I wanted Glenna to win. It was all right to hope for an American victory because that would make a better story, but this went beyond that. And for the first time also, as they played the thirteenth, I entertained the thought that Glenna might not win.

It is hardly proper to say that Miss Wethered had been let off the hook by that missed putt, but she must have been encouraged by that error after the way her opponent had been playing. She promptly holed a twelve- or fourteen-footer to win the 13th, and then got back two more holes before they finished the morning round. So the probable six up at the 12th had become only two up when we set out after lunch on the second journey around the course. Word of Joyce's recovery had got about the town, and the crowd now was large—ten thousand, they said, although that seems exaggerated. People were telling one another in jubilant voices loud enough for Glenna to hear, "She's only two doon noo". The match was turning right around as play progressed, and our girl's position was becoming desperate if not hopeless. I fought this thought all the way to the ninth, where Glenna had been five up only a few hours earlier. That seemed another match altogether when we came there again, for now she was four down with only nine to play. Over the fifteen holes from that unhappy morning turning-point, nine had been won by Miss Wethered. And Glenna had not given them away.

There was still to be some excitement. Glenna gave us hope by winning the 10th and 11th in 3s, and magnificent 3s they were. So she came to the fateful 12th only two down and seven holes left in which to get them back.

From this point in the morning, Miss Wethered had got back three, so it was entirely possible. Joyce went back to three up by winning the 13th, but she lost the 14th, the Long Hole In, to Glenna's par-5. What encouraged us here was that Glenna could have won the hole with an even bigger score, so poorly did Joyce play it. Then, at the 15th, the match reached its highest point of excitement and its climax.

This hole, a little more than 400 yards, shares an enormous green with the third hole, and its right edge is up against the railroad line. Miss Wethered, still apparently shaken by her experience at the 14th, sliced her drive, a rare thing for her. It ended up close to the rail line, and this prevented her from reaching the green. She played short of it and then left herself a putt of 18 or 20 feet with a half-flubbed run-up. This made four poor shots through the green on the last five holes. For the first time all day, she was not hitting the ball well.

Glenna meanwhile had followed a fine drive with a shot to the green with a wood, and then, with Joyce still so far away in three, she sensibly ran her ball close for her par 4. Only one down with three to play seemed certain now, and, with Miss Wethered playing so nervously, anything might happen. What did happen was that Miss Wethered holed the putt and undoubtedly won the match then and there, four holes from home. The putt was a really hard one, slightly uphill and over uneven ground. I would have given odds it could not be made, and even after she had struck the ball, I was sure it would not drop. She had hit it much too firmly, and it would have gone a long way past, but, of course, that was the only way to hit it. If the ball didn't go into the cup, it mattered not at all how far past it might go, since Glenna already was certain of her 4. It appeared to be another nervous stroke that Miss Wethered had played. The ball bounced a couple of times on its way, and I still do not quite see how it managed to get into the cup. Perhaps it can be explained by the fact that for the great ones or the ones favored by the gods these things seem to happen at critical moments, and you could cite a dozen cases in a dozen sports to prove it.

If you wanted Glenna to win though, it was hard to take, because, only a moment before the ball dropped, hope had flared. Miss Wethered may have thought herself lucky that Glenna had missed a three-foot putt at the 12th in the morning, but in the afternoon she created her own luck by running down a putt six times as long as the one Glenna had missed. Anyhow we all knew when it dropped that this was it, and the shout with which it was greeted showed that. Miss Wethered remained two up, and now she needed only a couple of halves for the match. There was a feeling that she was bound to get them, and one came immediately at the 16th, making her dormie two.

The crowd now was having trouble controlling itself. I followed well behind when the ladies had driven on the Road Hole, and, after seeing Glenna make two somewhat less than perfect shots, I worked my way through the throng and onto the road behind the green. It was obvious that, when the time came, this crowd was going to break and rush toward Miss Wethered, and I wanted to be well out of the way. I could not see them play out the hole, but this wasn't necessary. There was no doubt that this was the actual end, with Miss Wethered winning the 17th, or 35th, hole to close out the match, 3 and 1. I stood far back as the crowd, with a loud burst of cheering, rushed onto the green, sweeping players, caddies, and officials into a swirling mass. The two girls disappeared in a sea of people, and years passed before I saw either of them again.

I waited until I could walk along the road, then went

slowly, back to my room at the Grand. I felt depressed and didn't want to write the story. I don't see how it would have been possible not to want Glenna to win that match, and it was only prolonged contemplation of Miss Wethered's excellencies that brought the proper perspective. I had been gradually coming to a realization throughout the afternoon that Miss Wethered had won because she was the better player, and now I had to face that thought before sitting down to write of her victory. I had cared more than I had realized, but the evidence was in.

I sat for a long time in the late afternoon going over in my mind Joyce Wethered's wonderful shotmaking and trying to find words for it. I tried out such phrases as "serene and gracious swing", swiped from somewhere, and her "elegant and faultless style". (I can still picture to myself the perfection of those low-flying mashie shots and the dead certainty of those putts.) At the 17th green, just before the end, a spectator in front of me had said, "She's wi'oot maircy". Yes, nae maircy when the battle was joined but otherwise gentle, unpretentious and immensely popular. Most of these words of praise might also have been said of Glenna, and it occurs to me that there never have been two more attractive players and personalities to contest a championship.

For me, Miss Wethered remains the finest woman golfer I have seen. Those who did not see her may dispute this judgment, and I feel sure they will. Some will have it that Babe Zaharias was the best. Others will vote for Mickey Wright or some other of the terribly good girls on the tour. The record books will support them, and if you are going to argue these things, you have to lean on the record. Women's golf has changed so much since Miss Wethered's day that comparisons are difficult if not altogether useless. There was no women's professional golf at all in the playing sense then. The talented women golfers of that time, and there were a good many of them, played only one or two major tournaments a year. They played regularly if informally at their clubs, in their own sectional events and in the national championships. That was about it. The girls on the Ladies' PGA tour today actually play more big tournaments in one season than Joyce and Glenna played in their entire careers. This, in itself, indicates the tremendous changes that have come about.

The girls of the 1970s score sensationally, but scores do not tell everything, and I think both Glenna and Joyce would score with the champions if they were playing now. The golf we saw on the Old Course confirms this, I think. Glenna and Joyce were amateurs who played mostly for the pleasure of it, and yet their skills were at the professional level.

Perhaps not even Glenna and Joyce could play better golf than Babe Zaharias did in winning her last U.S. Open title at the Salem Country Club, in Peabody, Mass., in 1954 with a 72-hole score of 291, when she already was in the later stages of the cancer from which she died. They would be equally hard put to match Mickey Wright's performance in winning the same title at Baltustrol in 1961 with 293. I suspect that Miss Wright's third and fourth rounds on the final day, 69–72, were, in fact, the most dynamic golf played by a woman in my time in a championship event over such a long and difficult course.

Still, I think it took something comparable to beat Glenna that day at St. Andrews, and from the simple standpoint of striking the ball with various clubs and doing it beautifully, I think I must stick with Miss Wethered. She could drive the somewhat less lively ball with wooden-shafted clubs as far as they drive the ball in recent years, and she could make the ball "do" things that today's women's champions don't seem to know about at all. It should not be forgotten in this era of so-called power golf that Miss Wethered drove level with Bob Jones on many holes when they played together, and that she could get home with her second on holes somewhat longer than 500 yards. She did not have that useful club, the wedge, but she solved that problem by never getting into places where it would be needed.

I realize that I have seen comparatively little women's golf above the district level and that there are many women professionals I have not seen play. But I hold to my perhaps stubborn belief that Miss Wethered was the best, and I am bolstered in it by two pretty good men whose experience of lady golfers was more extensive than my own. Henry Cotton has said of Joyce, "In my time no golfer, male or female, has stood out so far ahead of his or her contemporaries," and Bob Jones, after playing a friendly foursome with Miss Wethered on the Old Course at St. Andrews before the British Amateur of 1930, testified in writing as follows: "She did not miss one shot. She did not even half-miss one shot, and when we had finished, I could not help saying that I never played with anyone, man or woman, amateur or professional, who made me feel so utterly outclassed. I have no hesitancy in saying she is the best golfer I have ever seen."

CHAPTER VII
THE MASTERS

At Augusta National, Jones left us a legacy perhaps greater and more enduring than the Grand Slam of 1930. His record will speak eloquently so long as golf is played, but statistics do not tell the whole story of a man who had been so much more than a champion golfer. Records fall and athletic achievement may easily be ignored or forgotten by those who come after. Jones gave his name to an era, but it is the Masters that should and probably will stand as his monument. The story of the Masters falls into three periods, the first ending with Pearl Harbor when the tournament was eight years old. The second period extends from the renewal of the tournament in 1946 into the 1950s, during which the event grew in delight and popular appeal. And, as the 1950s moved into the Great Golf Boom, they brought changes that ushered in a new period which happily continues. Today it is doubtful that any event in all of sport is comparable to the Masters if all the elements in it are taken into account.

It was during the early years of this third period that the phrase, "See you at the Masters", began to have magic in it. This happy incantation became common in the world of golf whenever prospective visitors parted company any time after the first of the year. It went at the bottom of letters and at the end of phone calls, for by then the Masters had cast its spell of excited anticipation over all who had come under its influence and all who hoped to.

We had come to know by heart the details of this magnetic tournament played always the first full week in April against Augusta's brilliant backdrop of flowering plants and bushes and towering pines. Golfers, golf spectators and readers of golf literature are, in regard to this annual fixture, like happy children who demand that a fairy tale be repeated over and over again in exactly the same way. It is only dull grown-ups and non-golfing peo-

ple who think a story, once told, is finished. The Masters
story is new every year, for it is itself a kind of fairy tale.

Any number of people have described the unique golfing experience of a first visit to the Masters. It is an experience that those who were on hand at the Masters early
and continuously can never have in the same way, since
the extravagance of the scenes developed gradually over
the years and all of us with them. Memory plays tricks on
us when an event becomes such an integral part of our
lives. It is impossible to sort out just when the Masters
ceased to be a great invitational tournament and became a
great national spectacle.

After 1968, Bob Jones no longer was physically present
during the playing of the Masters, but it still was his tournament and it still is though he is gone. Golf people
should not be allowed to forget that, and here I would like
to repeat for those with short memories or insufficient
years that huge golf galleries were not invented by Arnold
Palmer, whose "Army" first mustered in such enormous
numbers at Augusta. Remarkable as this response to
Palmer undoubtedly was, and is, there is something that
should be kept in mind: it does not compare with what
took place when Jones played. Nothing in the whole history of sport compares with the mounting tension that
built up around the world as that wonderful summer of
1930 moved from St. Andrews to Hoylake and to In-
terlachen en route to its climax at Merion, where Jones
completed both the Grand Slam and his own playing
career.

How many hundreds of thousands in how many lands
followed Jones's progress without benefit of television or
radio? How many millions who never were to see him
even on the screen felt a personal involvement with the
charming young lawyer who had stirred their hearts? This

cannot be calculated. No more could we explain the hold Jones still had on the hearts of the people everywhere long after he played his last tournament. Those seemingly long-ago triumphs of his are not pre-historic, and those of us who chronicled them and remained to tell of Arnie and his Army, of Jack Nicklaus and his tremendous feats, would be woefully inadequate historians if we did not tell the new generations of golfers and spectators what Bob Jones meant and still means, though he no longer lives.

During the last years of his playing career, Jones began to have recurring thoughts about a golf course that would embody the ideas he had developed while playing the famous courses here and abroad. He did not mention this at the time but spoke of it often in later years: how the Augusta National Golf Club happened to be founded, how the course he longed to build was built, and how his modest spring invitational tournament ultimately grew into one of the major championships.

The number of things which combined to produce this annual golf festival, in a setting so beautiful and so perfectly conceived, are too many to list. The people who worked hard to bring it about are known and have been properly praised, but obviously Jones's contribution overshadows all the rest. The intangibles he was responsible for are numberless. The spiritual overtones that derived from his mere presence are enormous. But, physically speaking, it all began with the course. The other things, tremendous in their way, were added later or came about as a natural result of Jones's being there. Without Jones the whole thing is unthinkable.

The Augusta National is Bob Jones's course; it is one of the great golf courses of the world; and it has had a profound influence on golf-course architecture. Jones, who wrote more clearly and more forcefully about the game than most of us who earn our living at it, has spoken often of how it all came about. In his book "Golf is My Game" (Doubleday), he says:

"I shall never forget my first visit to the property that is now the Augusta National. The long lane of magnolias, through which we approached, was beautiful. The old manor house, with its cupola and walls of masonry two feet thick, was charming. The rare trees and shrubs of the old nursery were enchanting. But when I walked out on the grass terrace under the big trees behind the house and looked down on the property, the experience was unforgettable."

How many persons have since had the same experience and reacted in the same way? Year after year, they come in their tens of thousands. In the years since 1931, there have been numberless changes made to the property. The old clubhouse has been added to, and new buildings of the same Southern Colonial style stretch right and left. Cabins have sprung up, and there is even an elegant par-3 course hidden away among the pines. But all these are behind you when you stand where Jones stood that day, and, as he said, you still "see the property exactly as I saw it then".

This vista from the top of the hill is the essential thing to keep in mind, for therein lies the very remarkable thing that Jones, with his co-architect, Alister Mackenzie, accomplished with this unusual piece of golfing ground. Probably nowhere else on a vast modern golf course is the work of man and machine less visible or the original scenic beauty of the landscape as well preserved. Nothing here is out of keeping with its surroundings.

The truly great golf courses of the world are those which have been "discovered", so to speak, rather than built. They were already hidden in the contours of the land before those who would build them came along.

Anyone with a bulldozer can make a golf course of sorts nearly anywhere by following what is on the drawing board. Courses of this genus we have in quantity. Some of them we may even like very much, but we should be wary of calling them great. If it is true that nearly anyone with the help of modern machinery can build a pretty good golf course, it is equally true that only nature can produce a great one. If it is not there in the land already, the cleverest golf architect in the world cannot bring it to life, although it does not necessarily follow that being there it is bound to be spotted. The talented architect, amateur or professional, is the one who both sees and reveals it. When an imaginative builder encounters favorable terrain, the conditions are right for a memorable achievement. Which brings us back to Augusta and to Jones and Mackenzie.

When these two men, one the world's finest golfer, the other a physician turned golf-course architect, first visited the old farm outside Augusta that had been a nursery for flowering trees, they stood on the terrace and looked out upon one of the fairest prospects in all the Southland. And together they saw a golf course sleeping beneath a canopy of majestic trees and flowering shrubs with streams wandering here and there.

It is possible to speak of a typical American course in a way that would be meaningless in Great Britain. The typical American course is on undulating meadowland, has many trees but little rough in the British sense, and is so well groomed that it resembles a park. Its bunkers and other hazards are nearly always clearly defined, and almost all the trouble is immediately visible. This is exactly the face that the Augusta National presents to the visitor. Why was it so revolutionary?

There was great interest throughout the world of golf during the building of the new course, and, as it neared completion, there arose an eagerness to see what the world's finest golfer had wrought. Mackenzie died not long after the course was completed, but the project had been known all along simply as "Bobby Jones's course down in Georgia", and the Scotsman never has received proper credit for his important part in it. At any rate, it was Jones who finally presented it for inspection early in 1933, and a number of things were immediately apparent.

First, it was clear that one of the finest jobs ever of fitting course to terrain had been achieved. The prospect from the hilltop was not less but more beautiful with the holes added, since Jones and Mackenzie had been working with largely cleared land requiring comparatively little earth-moving. It was also apparent, and it became increasingly so as one Masters followed another, how it is possible to build a golf course that challenges the expert and at the same time gives pleasure to the low-, middle-, and high-handicap golfers. All classes of players may be served, it seemed to say, without building mile-long teeing grounds and huge greens merely for the sake of bigness.

To many experienced players who inspected the new course, the scarcity of bunkers and the absence of rough were a surprise and a revelation. To accommodate the ordinary golfer—and most members of the Augusta National Golf Club were pretty average players—the course had to be wide open and comparatively free of man-made hazards. There were only twenty-odd bunkers on the course, fewer than two to a hole. The large undulating greens were protected by their own conformation, and the fairways were made testing principally by the banks and slopes of the ground itself and not by the occasional bunker. Obviously here was a course where the golfer looking to make a low score had to think of what he was going to do before he did it, since each shot determined the following one, making it easier or more difficult according to where the ball came to rest. The key to a low score was the shot to the greens. The greens were so constructed that the chances of getting the ideal angle on the approach could be improved or reduced by moving the pins to different positions. From the day the course was opened, the ordinary golfers found themselves scoring just about the same or a stroke or two lower than they did on their home courses, although the experts on the professional tour had to struggle hard for the birdies that came so easily elsewhere.

These were the basic facts about the new course, and they have remained basic through all the changes that have been made over the years. The Augusta National has evolved, to be sure, as the playing of the Masters and the coming of the huge crowds showed what could be done to increase the enjoyment of both golfer and spectator. Many small and subtle changes and a few large ones have turned an excellent course into an even better one. The first Masters field, incidentally, played the course the other way round. The original first hole is now the tenth, for Jones realized after studying the maiden Masters in 1934 that the dramatic qualities of future tournaments could be vastly enhanced if the two nines were reversed.

I do not think there is a single hole, unless it be the par-3 fourth, that remains exactly as we saw it in 1934. However, the whole scene "looks" the same. The major changes, aside from the revisions made on the course, have been for the purpose of serving the tournament's patrons better. They came in ever-increasing numbers until a limit had to be set. The best of spectator courses by intent and design, Augusta National has become ever more so as time has passed.

The Masters tournament has been fortunate that no individual or organization could profit from its large income, so funds have always been available for improving course and grounds. The money had to be spent, and the Augusta National is a club whose far-flung individual members do not average many rounds on the course each year. For this reason, changes have been more for the benefit of the tournament and the public than for the membership, but no change has been arbitrary. None has been made without due consideration and discussion, and none has intruded unduly on the natural contours and beauty of the land.

The excitement that grew up around the attempt of Bobby Jones, three years out of competitive golf, to come back in the first Masters, is difficult to recall, but it was so great that newspapers put it on page one as the first tournament, called then the Augusta National Invitation, approached. "Eyes of Nation On Augusta as Bobby Jones Makes Comeback", one old clipping announces. These were depression years, and golf, like everything else, was in the doldrums. The mere presence of Jones focussed attention on the new tournament and the new course, and for this reason alone the Augusta National quickly became known throughout the golf world. Jones's "comeback" and his tournament also gave golf a much needed shot in the arm, a fact, I think, that we are all a little too willing to forget.

The Augusta National had immediate star appeal. It had a character and a charm singularly its own, and there seems to have been something implicit in the design of the course that from the start invited and welcomed the spectacular. There is no golf course in my experience that so surely and so effectively produces the winning charge from behind or the losing collapse by a leader. Many thousands were to swarm over the course each year, millions soon were to see parts of it on TV, and it soon became the best-known and the most-photographed golf course in the world.

We may be sure that all the new and old architects of the 1960s and 1970s knew the Augusta National well and were conscious of its values as they went to work on their own courses. Many of them were influenced by its design and playing qualities, and, although some architects failed to get the full message, we were saved any real horrors. The average quality of golf-course construction was raised because of the Augusta National. It is the outstanding example in this country of strategic design, as opposed to punitive design, and it is so beautiful and has become so familiar to thousands that it has inevitably pointed the way to golf-course designers, just as the management of the club and the tournament have shown how a golf event can and should be run.

After demonstrating that a golf course may just as well be built with spectators, expert tournament players, and ordinary club members all in mind, the Masters was the first to show that a big crowd, moving too freely for its size, endangers the game, and that the old rules of spectator control were obsolete. It was at Augusta that the USGA learned a good deal about crowd control and many other things about tournament procedure, some of which have unfortunately been ignored.

In the early days of the Masters and even for a while after the war, you could mingle with and speak to the players on the course and about the grounds, even chat with Bobby Jones himself without benefit of marshals. And when the coming of the hordes made it necessary to keep spectators off the course by roping the fairways, a good deal of the old intimacy was retained. The crowds still do mingle with and speak to the players as at no other golf event. That a spectacle so huge should keep even a little of its early intimacy is something of a golfing miracle.

That broad green terrace behind the clubhouse, where
Jones and Mackenzie first stood to sweep the scene, still is
there, with the large practice putting green on a lower
terrace just beyond. During Masters week this terrace becomes a sort of Village Green of Golf. At this delightful
meeting place under the trees, seemingly as old as time,
all the modern participants in this ancient game happily
convene. Here come officials of all district golf associations up and down the land to meet with their kind and to
learn how golf tournaments should be run. With them
come every sponsor and every promoter. Each one
would, if he could, make his own tournament a duplicate
of the Masters. Here, too, come manufacturers of golf
equipment of all kinds, not to hawk their wares but to
meet with all the other people of the game they serve and
which serves them. And here come the old Open and
PGA champions, for the Masters invites them back as
guests each year to lend their presence and bring still
another dimension no other tournament has. And all
these people who make the game what it is throughout
the country—the sponsors, officials, manufacturers, old
champions and current heroes—are not insulated from
the crowds at Augusta. They *are* the crowd. Outside the
ropes they mingle with the people who come to watch,
and all flow together in the most homogeneous gathering
in all sport.

Sitting on this terrace, with every element of the modern game of golf eddying about, it is possible to relive
one's whole golfing life. In spite of its quality of being a
great public spectacle, in spite of the changes that come
with time, in spite of everything, at the Masters one still
gets the *feel* of the game as such. This huge show really
does connect us with the past, with the game that we
knew when we were young.

There developed among the writers who were latecomers to the Masters scene a tendency to belittle the whole affair. That seemed to distress Clifford Roberts, the tournament Chairman, but it never bothered Jones at all. Bob forgave them, as he said, because the event had received so much praise by the time of their arrival, there was little left to say. Praising the Masters had become a good deal like commending the liquidity of water. Criticism had become about the only way to attract attention. The easiest, quickest and cheapest way to make a small score is to attack the establishment, to knock down something others praise, something the multitude admires. These voices of dissent have gone largely unheard because they attacked the wrong things. The rest of us, whose tongues had been filled with praise from the start, also found things to criticize as the tournament grew, and I cannot think of a single reasonable suggestion in all the years that was not accepted by Jones and Roberts.

Jones played in each tournament from 1934 to 1948. He played with the same precise technique, "without hesitation and without ambiguity", and with the old beauty of his lazy, almost dreamlike swing. But more and more as the years advanced the old command was lacking. What his presence meant, his playing in the tournament when all chance of his winning was out of the question, should not be underestimated. He gave the event in its early years, and later, a distinction and a flavor no other golf gathering ever had.

After Jones's declining health forced him to give up playing in the Masters, the tournament retained the aura he had given it. Even after he was stricken, he would come each day from his white cabin beyond the tenth tee, climb painfully into his cart and drive about the course. It was an effort because he never was free from pain, but it was an effort he made gladly because of the pleasure it gave him and also because of a sense of duty toward the tournament he had created. As tournament followed tournament through the 1950s, he at length became so crippled he could no longer handle a cart. Then he was driven by Roberts, the man in whose hands he left the club, course and tournament when he was no longer able to be present in person.

Roberts, a New York investment banker, was one of the organizers of the Augusta National, and he subsequently handled the multifarious details of setting up the new spring tournament while Jones busied himself with the course and the major decisions. Actually, Roberts ran the tournament from the beginning as far as its intricate operation and management were concerned, and he handled these matters with such a firm touch, making improvements each time the event was held, that he became the shrewdest and most efficient tournament director the game had known. But always there was Jones's influence and overall direction. He was *the* decision-maker, the one whose word was final. This was, however, a happy collaboration from the start. The coming together of Jones and Roberts was as critical for the tournament as the meeting of Jones and Mackenzie had been for the course. It was of great value to the tournament that it was Roberts who drove Jones about the course when Bob could no longer manage this himself. They would stop here and there at a favorite spot to watch the golfers come by. Each time Roberts would stop, people who had known Bob in other days would come up to pay their respects. Others who didn't know him personally would stand a little way off, very conscious of him. They liked to look at him from a certain distance and feel they were in his presence.

I was witness to these little scenes many times, and often I would stand at a little distance myself and watch with a conjunction of feelings. I noticed that even old friends of Jones's, unwilling now to subject him to the strain of a personal visit, would watch and wait for the chance to have a few words with him. Invariably there was genuine joy and gladness in their greeting and, there is no other word for it, a certain reverence in their attitude. It was good to see that even in those who stood apart and were unable to come up, there was something of the same feeling, and it was a deep satisfaction to me to realize that there were many people who felt the right way about Bob Jones.

Because of the very nature of the Masters, it seemed as if almost the whole world of golf was witness to, even participated in, the slow decline of the game's finest player and greatest personality—first one cane, then two, then the cart followed by the wheelchair, and finally no Bob Jones at the Masters.

CHAPTER VIII
A SINGULAR MAN:
BEN HOGAN

In the decades before television and commercial sponsorship began to innundate golf with money, there were certain tests unrelated to earnings that a player was asked to pass to be accepted among the game's great players. He was expected to win the U.S. Open more than once and remain near the top of the Open for a number of years; he was asked to win repeatedly in the week-long match-play championships; and he was required to win on both sides of the Atlantic when that meant taking about a month off from the tournament schedule in this country. These criteria held good only through what has been called the Age of Hogan, which somewhat overlapped the new era of the millionaire PGA Tour player.

Of the golfers I followed and wrote about during that earlier period, there were four I admitted to the highest rating from the point of view of style, shotmaking, personality and achievement. Three of them, Walter Hagen, Bob Jones and Gene Sarazen, we have dealt with. The other was Ben Hogan. His records, and very likely theirs, probably will be eclipsed—many already have been—but I very much doubt that any of us will ever see a better golfer. I did not enjoy with Hogan the warm personal relationship I had with the others, but I am convinced that even in the sixth decade of his life he was the best striker of the ball alive.

I first encountered Ben Hogan not long before World War II brought an end to that long string of beautiful summers in Britain that had begun with Jones at Sunningdale in 1926. Hogan was slowly fighting his way up from the obscurity of the same Texas caddie yard from which Byron Nelson had emerged to become one of the game's leading players. Nelson, about the same age and from the same background, was in 1937 already playing on the Ryder Cup team in England the very week that Hogan resigned his job at the Oakhurst Club in Fort

Worth in order to go on the tour. Ben said he had saved $1400 and had to take the big gamble then or never.

The story of Hogan's struggle now is well known, but few paid it attention early on, and I was not among them. It wasn't until 1946 that he gained close national attention by winning the PGA championship, which in those days was a tough six-day match-play affair. Behind Hogan were three years of service in the Army Air Corps and endless months of post-war practice during which the chronic hook that had plagued him from the beginning became the controlled fade that was to help usher him into the select company of the truly great.

Actually, the moment when Ben first gained national acceptance as a true champion came at the Riviera Country Club, in Los Angeles, in June of 1948. There Ben won the first of his four Open titles with the lowest score—67-72-68-69—276—ever recorded. He did it on the longest course, 7020 total yards, on which the Open had been played. This was eight strokes below par on a course arbitrarily reduced to par 71 precisely for the purpose of preventing a winning score too far below the standard figure. It was a significant score which led to a significant decision. It first called the attention of the USGA to the necessity of adjusting older golf courses to modern golf equipment, and it had a major bearing on the Ben Hogan story.

Hogan also won the PGA Championship for a second time that year and apparently had reached the top of his form. He was regarded as the country's leading golfer, replacing Nelson, the wartime leader, but he was not a popular champion. People found him blunt, tight-lipped, steely-eyed and cold; a man of much talent but little appeal. All that was changed on a fog-shrouded West Texas highway in February of 1949. That is where the real Ben Hogan story begins. Ben was returning to Fort Worth from a tournament in Phoenix. His car crashed head-on into a bus, leaving him, we all thought, crippled for life and done with golf forever.

Among his injuries were a double fracture of the pelvis, a broken collar bone, a broken bone in the left ankle and broken ribs. An operation to save his life and prevent blood clots was performed, and the large veins in both legs had to be tied off. The story now becomes so much like fiction even Hollywood toned down the more incredible parts. As often as it is told, it will seem incredible for those of us who, lacking these qualities, admire greatly the courage, fight, will and desire that Hogan displayed. A wave of sympathy swept the country for this man and for his wife, Valerie, who was saved, as we all knew, from serious injury, perhaps death, when Ben threw his own body across hers in the last instant before the crash. It was not only the world of golf that was saddened.

We thought for a while that Ben would not live. Then we were told that he would not walk again, and we knew that he would never again play golf. For fifty-nine days he remained in a hospital in El Paso, and the reports were not encouraging. In April, when he was moved to his home in Fort Worth, Ben was a shadow of a man whose body had been cruelly broken. Operations on the legs had apparently left them permanently swollen.

Some few weeks later, word came that Hogan had taken a few steps, and, after a while, we learned that he was actually walking about, though with difficulty and pain. Hogan's will was at work full time. The next word was that Hogan was hitting golf balls and, later still, that he had played a few holes. Finally and incredibly, toward the end of the summer, he announced that he intended to play tournaments again.

It was preposterous to those who had known how badly Hogan had been injured, but on the morning of

January 5, 1950, eleven months after the accident, a large
crowd around the first tee of that same Riviera Golf Club
responded with a burst of cheering to one of the most
electrifying announcements a golf gallery ever heard:
"Ben Hogan, on the first tee, please".

This was not the same Hogan. It was a slimmer, almost
gaunt Hogan with legs encased in heavy rubber stockings
and a stiff, limping walk in which there was a good deal
of pain. And a different Hogan in other ways, too. Gone
was at least a part of the cold, indifferent, remorseless
Hogan, consumed in the fires of the ordeal through which
he had passed. This was a Hogan who could smile and
respond to public acclaim, and, as was soon to be seen, an
even better golfer than before despite—or, perhaps, because of—the suffering and handicaps he had overcome.

Hogan had been given the designation of "Honorary
Starter", but his response to that had been, "Honorary,
hell! I'm playing". This was the new Hogan speaking
without the old venom. He forced his aching body to go
the full four-day route of the L.A. Open, and, when all
the scores were in, it had taken two birdie putts by Sam
Snead to tie Hogan for first. That he later lost the playoff
became incidental. Hogan was back, and back on the front
pages. We did not know what lay ahead. Some florid
prose describing Hogan "the comeback king of all time"
greeted the feat at Riviera, but Hogan himself said this
was no comeback. His real comeback effort was pointed
toward the U.S. Open in June. I think many felt sorry for
Ben when they heard this. Physically the Open, with its
36-hole grind on the final day, was too much for him. And
Merion, a classic course, was bound to be extremely demanding mentally and physically. We did not want to see
him struggle, suffer and fail. But Hogan gave us one of
the great stories in golf history to write, and if we had

risen to it as he rose to the occasion, we might all have been prize winners.

Not much else but Hogan mattered at Merion. His progress around the course was painfully slow. He limped badly on his rubber-encased legs which required treatment after each round, but when the third round began on Saturday morning he was only two strokes behind the leader, Dutch Harrison. Asked if his legs would stand the punishment of two rounds that day, Hogan made a reply that none there will forget. "Don't worry about me," he said. "When I come up the 18th fairway the second time, you'll think you're seeing another Jesse Owens."

This was the new Hogan speaking. The old one might have just called it a damn silly question and not answered. Tens of thousands will never forget how dramatic his late-afternoon journey up the 18th, or 72d, fairway was.

Merion had taken its toll of every golfer in contention that long day, and when Hogan came to the 18th tee after walking some ten miles since breakfast, that subtle magic which attends these moments in golf hung over the course. Lloyd Mangrum and George Fazio were tied for the lead at 287, and Hogan needed a par 4 on this 458-yard finishing hole to join them in a three-way tie.

He, too, had dropped strokes that might have won for him, and now at the end he had to hit two perfectly directed full shots and get down in two putts to stay alive. The possibility that he might still win with a birdie certainly was there, but even a par 4 was very hard to come by on this dangerous and difficult hole. The other possibility, a 5, was also in our minds. Hogan hit a perfect drive, straight and far, and now came the most important shot of the tournament. Most players had taken a wooden club to this green, but Hogan chose a 2-iron. More than 10,000, they say, watched the shot. They lined each side of the fairway, were massed around the green, and were closed in on the fairway behind him. Without ropes to hold the gallery bank, it is a wonder they gave him room to swing.

When the 2-iron shot rose from the turf, they broke and ran for the green, shutting it and the flying ball from sight. Hogan knew it was home. It was a superlative shot. It finished some thirty-five feet from the hole. It set up the par-4 he needed to tie the leaders, and it also set up Hogan's second victory on the Open.

The playoff, as so often happens, was an anti-climax except for the thrill of knowing that Hogan crowned his comeback by giving death a steady and courageous look in the eye, in the best possible way. The galleries had seen this wonderfully appealing story rise to its climax, and they rejoiced. Overnight Hogan had revived, and in the playoff, his 69 enabled him to win by four strokes over Mangrum and by six over Fazio. It was on the 16th green of the playoff that Mangrum, himself a former champion, took the famous two-stroke penalty for thoughtlessly lifting his ball to blow off a bug.

A little while after the finish, the new Hogan came up the steps to the stiflingly inadequate press quarters. He was mightily pleased and mightily tired, and both things could be seen in the face that once had concealed almost everything. He was more than just affable now. He said: "You fellows have been good to me. Real nice. But I'm damn tired of being called an invalid. I wish you wouldn't write it any more."

So we gave him his wish. At least I did, and I never used the "Bantam Ben" label that others gave such a good workout because I sensed he did not care for that either.

The return of the newer and greater Hogan to the golf scene was confirmed when he won the Masters the next April. Here Ben, starting late on the last day and knowing what he had to do, did it with an efficiency that was so convincing no one could miss it. It also was here at Augusta that spring of 1951 that a subtle change in Hogan's manner was noticed, and I think that a manifestation of it was that the name "The Hawk" was first applied to him there. With his return to the top, Ben seemed to move back a little toward the old Hogan. A little of the old coldness began to come through again along with just a touch of the old indifference, but it was softer and without the old disdain.

The name, The Hawk, seemed appropriate there at Augusta and even more appropriate two months later when he waited on the first tee at Oakland Hills, outside Detroit, to begin what may have been the most praiseworthy round of golf the Open has known. I think of it as the finest single Open round that I've seen in a lifetime of walking the best courses in the world with some of the most gifted champions. One does not, however, think of flawlessness in this case. Instead, it was the successful outcome of a three-day battle of wits with a course arbitrarily doctored for the purpose of making the mighty fall. At Merion and Riviera, it had been Hogan against an array of almost equally talented golfers. At Oakland Hills, it was the golfers against the golf course, and in the end it was Hogan against what he called the Monster. Only Hogan found the way to deal with it, and even he needed three rounds of confusion and worry before the Monster, at the very end, was made to yield. No other Open championship in memory has presented a comparable situation.

Ben seemed tired and still a little worried as he came to

the first tee in early afternoon on Saturday to play his final
round on a perfect summer's day. Three rounds were
behind him now—he had played the third that morning—
and the championship was still up for grabs. Not one
golfer in the starting field of 162 had as yet shot a score
below par. By narrowing the fairways and adding pun-
ishing and questionable hazards, the course had been
made so difficult that no one in the entire field of fine
players had been able to come to terms with it in the first
fifty-four holes. These changes had been based on obser-
vations and measurements made by Robert Trent Jones,
the leading architect of the day. The idea was to make par
mean something once again, and this all went back to
Hogan's record low score at Riviera in the 1948 Open.
Obviously they had overdone things, and there had been
a good deal of moaning and indignant denunciation.

Hogan had not complained. While the others moaned,
he accepted the situation. He had been studying the
course, sparring with it, probing here, attacking there,
yielding when forced to do so. At the start of the final day,
fifteen players were listed ahead of him on the scoreboard, and five strokes separated him from Bobby Locke,
the British Open champion, who led with 144. Hogan had
still to stalk the giant through a long day's play on legs
that were still painful. He was an early starter, and the
sun had hardly burned the dew from the grass when it
seemed the Monster might be ready for slaying. The Monster only reeled, he did not fall. He fought back, and at
lunch time Hogan still had ground to make up, although
his score and his position had improved with every
round. With a grudgingly accepted 71 after his first two
rounds of 76 and 73, his 221 was two strokes behind Locke
and Jimmy Demaret. Also ahead of him were Julius Boros
and Paul Runyan, and close behind a dozen possible
winners.

When Ben placed his ball on the first tee in front of the clubhouse that afternoon, with people stretched away as far as visibility extended, it meant nothing to him that, being an early starter, he would not know what the players with lower scores were doing. He knew now what score would win. Some of us were thinking sadly that on his morning round, which had begun so hopefully, Ben had let slip his chance to join the three-time winners of the Open. He stood before his ball for a brief moment on the first tee, and got set for his opening drive with hardly a waggle. One final look into the distance, and the driver moved with that familiar build-up of power on the wide arc of the back-swing. Then, with almost no pause at the top, came the searing impact of clubhead on ball, which was swept away between the long lines of eager faces and craning necks. Then the long, upright follow-through. The fateful round had begun. Through the hot afternoon we followed him, attending his every move, patient with delay, and in us rose the feeling of connoisseurship from being able to appreciate what was so far beyond our powers to perform. Within us grew a kinship with the performer, the artist. Slowly at first, then overwhelmingly, came the feeling that we were part of a historic occasion.

The first nine, however, was still stubborn, not yet ready to yield, and Hogan was not yet ready to insist. A stroke was lost instead of gained at the short third. We could not know it then, but this was the last misdirected shot we would see Ben Hogan hit that afternoon. That stroke still was lost, though, when we arrived at the 7th, a par-4 of 381 yards.

Now, for the first time, it seemed that Ben opened his shoulders as he hit from the tee. A magnificent drive, long and perfectly placed, brought loud exclamations of delight and wonder. It is easy to forget that Hogan was one of the longest hitters when he wanted to be. Undoubtedly there had been something extra in this drive, and, as he had approached the ball, a certain tension had risen in us. It is one of the unaccountable things about a huge crowd at a golf championship that it can anticipate what may be just ahead. We were prepared for what now occurred. Hogan played a 7-iron, and those behind him could see the ball rise and begin to fall on the green, but they could not see where it fell. No need to see. Those who were at the green told us with a loud burst of shouts. We walked on and saw the ball two feet from the pin. The lost stroke had been made up, and eleven holes remained to be played.

We knew well that no one took liberties with the 8th, a par-4 of 458 yards that plays as a par-5 for members, and it was a relief to see that critical second putt go down. The walk from the eighth green to the ninth tee lay over a small hill and down a slight slope. On the left was the 11th green and 12th tee, and the flat section of this area, about the size of a city lot, was the most favorable spot on the course for watching the golfers come and go. Now as Hogan and his playing partner, Dave Douglas, moved through a path the marshals made for them toward the ninth tee, the crush was so feverish that people were being pushed down the slope on all sides. As we waited there for the pair ahead to clear the green, Locke passed down the first fairway close by on the right. We were surprised to see that he had some people with him. It seemed strange that there could be interest at this moment in anyone but Hogan. We reflected that Locke still would be two strokes ahead, though, if he arrived where we stood in par.

Every stroke had become terribly important. Hogan's 4-wood tee-shot on the ninth, a testing par 3, finished on the severly contoured green but so far from the cup that two putts seemed a certainty, and indeed they were. So

Hogan had made the turn in 35 and now faced the rough passage down the second nine.

The tenth is a strong par-4 of 448 yards to a hilltop green. The tee is on a broad terrace before the clubhouse, and the crush around and behind it when Hogan arrived there made movement out of the question. The ground drops quickly away to a fairway, set well below both the tee and the hilltop green. Hogan was out about 260 yards, a little to the right side, beyond one bunker but short of two others—no doubt just where he intended to be. While he waited, Hogan stood behind his ball, right arm folded, left elbow resting upon it, left arm moving back and forth ferrying that ever-present cigarette to his mouth. This was a familiar pose, and it was reassuring because it was the one Hogan assumed when he was most confident. He fastened his eyes on the flag somewhat less than 200 yards away. He spoke to the caddie and took the club without looking at it. We strained forward to see its number, and those in front whispered the word back that it was a 2-iron. He took a practice swing as he stood behind the ball. When he struck that shot, you could have taken a ruler and drawn a line from where it lay to where it came to rest four feet from the cup. This was a golf shot in which the ball did exactly what the striker intended. Later Hogan called it his best shot of the tournament: "It went exactly as I played it every inch of the way."

The roar which began as the ball rose in its flight became a vast explosion of sound from those banked around the green and then tapered off into excited babble as thousands of us raced to see if that key putt would go down. The time needed to measure it and remove invisible objects from its path—the whole process called reading the green—took an eternity. It is a wonder people did not go mad and scream as he stood motionless for so long over the ball. But when at last the putter did move, those close enough saw at once that the ball would enter the center of the cup. The roar began before the ball fell in, and when it did, a new note was heard in the voice of the crowd. It was a note almost of triumph, even this far from home. A subtle difference had taken place in both Hogan and the spectators.

Hogan did not have the power to inspire the affection that other crowds have felt for Ouimet and Jones and Palmer, but he possessed to a high degree the power to create tension. Outwardly nothing much changed in his manner, but the difference was there to feel if not to see. As he moved along toward the climax, waiting without impatience at each hole for the crowd to give him room to play, a certain ruthlessness began to creep in, faintly domineering. We began to feel that we could approach the climax with a feeling of confidence. Hogan himself seemed certain of victory. The pars came easily at the 11th and the par-5 12th, 566 yards long, and then, at the 169-yard 13th, he stopped a 6-iron fourteen feet from the stick. And here he gave us complete confidence by sinking the putt. Two under par for the tournament now. Our spirits soared only to sink again when he took a bogey 5 on the 14th. It was not a really bad shot that brought about the extra stroke. Here the safe route is hideously narrow, and the approach, seemingly perfect, rolled a few inches too far and found a bad spot. We had reached the extremity of the course now and were just about at the extremity of our emotions. We wondered if Hogan, standing now on the 15th tee, had not been shaken too by that 5.

The 15th was rated one of the easier par-4s, but on such a course that was not saying much. It still had to be played carefully. Only 392 yards long, a little dogleg left, it asked for a well-placed drive and a careful pitch to a raised green. On his morning round, Hogan had pushed his drive into the rough on the right, hooked his recovery from a very bad lie back across the fairway into the rough on the left, and, even worse, had then dumped his pitch from the stubbly rough into the bunker before the green. That double-bogey 6 was at the front of everyone's mind as Hogan prepared to play the fifteenth on his final round. This time his drive with his 4-wood sailed so far and so safely that no more than a soft pitch was needed to drop the ball over the bunker near the pin and to then hole the short putt for a birdie 3. Here was a champion's reply to a challenge.

The way Hogan played the dangerous 16th made everyone in the huge gallery certain he would win. As we hurried toward the tee, there came over the grapevine, which operated on championship courses before there were scoreboards everywhere, the news that only Clayton Heafner of the players in contention was staying close to par.

The 16th is a fabulous hole. Called the Lake Hole, the approach was the most dangerous shot on the course. Only 405 yards in length by the shortest route, the 16th has a fairway that bends around the left edge of a small lake. The green is a triangular peninsula that juts into the lake. Behind the green is a cluster of bunkers, and the green has a ridge running across its center. The second shot must carry over the small lake, and for most people going directly for the pin is foolhardy. Many balls had splashed into the lake in the early rounds even when the pin was set in a safer position on the left side of the green. Now the flag was positioned far to the right corner of the green where the danger was maximized. Nearly everyone elected to play conservatively to the left of the green and to try to get down in a chip and a putt for par. However, on his morning round, Hogan, after his double-bogey on the 15th, had bravely smacked his approach straight for the flag, set on the dangerous right side of the green. The ball had stopped only a few feet away. He had holed the putt for a birdie.

On his final round, Hogan again went straight for the flag. The ball once more pulled up a few feet from the cup. It had been almost an exact duplicate of the morning's shot. Hogan gave the impression he could repeat it a hundred times without the slightest variation. Nothing more was needed to convince us even when the putt did not go down this time. The 17th, a tough par 3 of 194 yards, had a steeply elevated green. Hogan played the hole perfectly and was two under par for the round with one hole left to go.

As he prepared to drive from the elevated tee of the seventy-second hole, a slight breeze was blowing behind him, and we wondered if he would try to get past the angle of the dogleg where the fairway turns right for the slight sweep upward to the green and the clubhouse. Many had failed in this endeavor, for in the angle there was thick rough, bushes, and some small trees. As we pondered these matters, Ben cut loose with his biggest drive of the day, flying the ball over a cluster of bunkers at the edge of the fairway and fading it around the corner. He was holding a 6-iron when he reached the ball, confident as soon as he had struck the drive that he would not need any more club than that.

The crowd had now become a mob, a surging mob eager for the kill. Joseph C. Dey, the USGA Executive Director, called it "the largest gallery in American golf history" and estimated it at more than 15,000 people. Hogan waited for the people to get done with their scrambling for position, and then waited for Douglas to shoot. Poor Dave Douglas! He had suffered the fate of all who play the last round with the champion and are not themselves in contention. He had been ignored. Nobody cared about Douglas. No one will remember that he finished fourth. Finally the time came, and there was a hush as Hogan played his approach. The ball rose very high, lost its impetus, and fell dead fourteen feet from the cup. Too far away for a birdie no doubt, but Ben did not need one now.

As Hogan came up to the green with the slightly waddling walk that had been forced upon him by his accident, Locke was standing on the nearby tenth tee. He had taken 37 strokes to the turn, and if Hogan now took two putts, Locke would have to play the treacherous last nine holes in 33 to tie. And then, while Locke waited, Hogan putted. The ball came to the cup on the high side, caught the corner, dropped in, and a wonderful 67 was duly achieved. People shrieked and roared and rushed onto the green. Hogan grinned a genuine, almost tearful grin showing how human a man he was after all.

When there was a little quiet, Locke turned, sadly it seemed, to drive his ball down the tenth fairway. He was now in the same position with the same score Hogan had two hours earlier at the same halfway point of the final round. But what a difference now. Locke's task still was possible when he birdied the tenth. It became impossible at the short 13th where, gambling to drop his 6-iron close to the pin, he found a front bunker instead. He brought in a 73 and finished third at 291, four strokes more than Hogan's winning 287.

A lot of the afternoon still remained, and it seemed to creep slowly toward dusk. One by one, the last players on the course gave up the chase, and, when they were finally in with their scores, the spectators gathered on the lawn for the presentation ceremony. Of the hundreds of rounds played that week, only one other than Hogan's had been below par. That was Heafner's closing 69, and it placed him second two strokes behind the champion.

After listening to the speeches at the presentation ceremony and taking back the cup he already owned, Hogan was handed the microphone. He stood silently for a little while, grasping it in both hands. Everyone was eager to hear what the champion would say after such a tournament and such a round. For a few moments, Hogan seemed unable to speak, much as a man is sometimes unable to move while standing frozen over a critical putt. Then he said: "I am glad that at last I was able to bring this monster to its knees."

This was indeed a monster of a golf course, probably the most difficult on which the Open had been played, and it had finally been mastered, the back nine ripped apart. As he stood there that evening, Hogan could survey the whole golfing world and find nowhere his equal as golfer, nowhere a course that could resist him.

It also is revealing to know a champion in defeat, and the picture of Hogan as loser does nothing to diminish his stature. Going into the 1952 Open at Northwood in Dallas, Ben had won three titles in three attempts. It is my belief that if the tournament had been played at Oakmont or on any championship course in the East or mid-West, Hogan very likely would have won it, and so would have owned, with his upcoming addition of the 1953 title, five consecutive Open victories. It was his misfortune that the USGA took the championship to his home state in 1952.

At Dallas he was beaten by the heat, which remained high in the 90s each day of that dreadful week and frequently soared above 100. And yet, in these debilitating conditions which wilted even the young players, this still partly crippled man played 69s the first two days when single rounds were played. In the whole history of the Open, no one ever had done a better 36-hole score, and Hogan led Julius Boros, the eventual winner, by four strokes. And when the final day's play began, Hogan seemed perfectly capable of doing two more 69s. This was deceptive. The heat already had taken its cumulative toll. He needed ten more strokes, two 74s, on the last two rounds played on that blistering Saturday. Boros, young and very strong, finished 68-71 for 281, an excellent score made possible by his ability to get down in two from a high number of greenside bunkers. Hogan was third with 285.

On the Monday following the tournament, I went with my brother, Dent Laney, a longtime resident of Fort Worth, to the Colonial Country Club in that city. There in the air-conditioned grill room we found Hogan at a table with Marvin Leonard, his friend and former sponsor, who had built the club. Invited to pull up chairs, we soon were discussing the Open. I remarked that it had been a great disappointment that Hogan had not won. I wanted very much to write of four in a row. Hogan looked steadily at his strong hands folded on the table for what seemed a full minute. Then his expression softened. When he looked up, amusement showed in his face and there was a suggestion of a twinkle in his eye.

"Oh," he said, "so *you* were disappointed. Ain't that too bad?"

When I spoke of the heat factor, he brushed it quickly aside, indicating clearly that he did not accept excuses for failure, but then he added that he did not think the Open should be played anywhere in the Southwest in June. There was sure to be excessive and continuous heat. He went on to say, with a sly look at his friend Leonard and a twitching of lips, "Anyhow, now the USGA's got those damn Texans off their necks for another twenty years."

Hogan is thought to be humorless, but there is plenty of it there when he wants to let it show. A little later, he returned to the subject of Oakmont. The old look came back to the cold but expressive and attractive face. "You said I would have won if it had been at Oakmont," he noted. "Well, it will be at Oakmont next year."

The next year was 1953, Hogan's finest, as 1930 had been Jones's. Ben put the seal on his greatness as conclusively as Jones had done with the Grand Slam. In April he won the Masters with the best golf he ever played throughout any tournament I witnessed. I do not think anyone will dispute the statement that Hogan's rounds of 70-69-66-69—274 at Augusta represent the most nearly flawless four rounds of golf ever played under championship conditions on one of the world's best courses. Oakmont, which was host to the Open that year, is another championship test. Hogan began with 67 and led at the end of every round. Finishing 3-3-3 on his fourth round, he was five under par for the championship and six ahead of Sam Snead in second place.

A couple of weeks after the Masters, I was covering a tournament at the lovely Whitemarsh club outside Philadelphia. I think it was the culmination of a cross-country match that Fred Corcoran had arranged for the women professionals. On the last day, Bob Harlow took me aside and said he was certain Hogan would go to Carnoustie for the British Open. But, I protested, he may not win at Oakmont and then he won't go.

"Oh, he knows he'll win at Oakmont," Bob said. "He'll go all right. If I had a daily paper to write for, that's the way I'd write it."

That's the way I wrote it, and that's the way it turned out. Looking back now, it seems to me it was the reluctance of some of us to regard Hogan as highly as we did Jones that caused him to make this effort so dangerously attended by the possibility of failure. To win in Great Britain was the one thing Jones had done and he hadn't. When he returned, Hogan, like Jones, had won four U.S. Opens and had shown in a sensational performance that he could win on both sides of the Atlantic. (He had earlier passed the match-play test easily.) Unlike Jones, he did not retire after his peak performance. He was, after all, a professional. Playing golf was his business, and when he arrived at Baltusrol for the 1954 Open, he appeared to be in full possession of his remarkable powers. That was the Open won by Ed Furgol, the appealing man with the withered arm, when Gene Littler and Dick Mayer, two future champions, failed to overhaul him on the final hole. Hogan was tied with four others six strokes back, but, in spite of this, Ben came to the Olympic Club in San Francisco in June of 1955 still rated by all of us as the man to beat. And how right we were!

Where Baltustrol was a club loaded with golf history after hosting ten national championships, the Olympic Club's Lake Course started the week of the Open in 1955 with no history at all in a national sense. By Sunday night, it had taken its place among the famous Open sites, for one of the most exciting dramas in American golf had been enacted there. The Lake Course, very difficult and very beautiful, was an unusual one on which to hold the Open. Although practically beside the Pacific Ocean, it winds through heavily wooded areas of lovely pines and cedars and eucalyptus. Near but not in sight of the Pacific, the course also runs along Lake Merced. Strong winds blow over the club's Ocean course, which, practically speaking, is just across the road, but the trees form a solid break for the Lake Course and they produce a strange effect. The wind blew mightily at times and sounded fierce. You heard it all around you, but you did not feel it much. This was so striking that it was noted immediately by all of us. Less obvious but also noted was another peculiarity: the fairways and greens were constantly "watered" by San Francisco's famous fog,

which came rolling in each night. There were other
things that might have explained what was to come, but
we failed to note them. Hogan could have shown them to
us, of course. It was, as always, fascinating to study his
specific preparations for a tournament, and never more
so than at Olympic.

We saw immediately on the practice days that Ben had
altered his swing and his manner of striking the ball. The
swing had become flatter and shorter. The usual sweeping, upright follow-through that had done the job so
many times was gone. In our ignorance we thought Ben
had adjusted his game to his own physical limitations and
that he was at last playing with impaired weapons. We
ought to have known better, to have understood that he
was adjusting to the new conditions just as he had at
Carnoustie. And when he had studied and tested the
course, I think that Hogan felt certain he could win a
record fifth U.S. Open. Everything indicated that he was
quietly confident, but the whole thing was over before we
really understood what had happened. It now seems
likely that of all the thousands who came to observe, to
play, to officiate and to report, only Hogan really knew
how the Lake Course should be played when the tournament began that Thursday morning in June, 1955.

What Hogan knew beforehand, what the rest of us did
not, was that length could be achieved only at a risk that
would be fool-hardy. He saw that the grass in the rough
was of a grasping, bunchy type never before encountered
on an Open course, and he was not among those surprised when it turned out to be tougher and more pun-
ishing than it looked to be. It also was permitted to en-
croach too closely around the greens, taking from the
golfers that wonderfully delicate shot from off the edge
that had been such a valuable part of Walter Hagen's
game. You simply couldn't judge how the ball would be-

have when you chipped it out of the thick growth of rough bordering the greens. A man might play a long iron or wood to these greens and have it roll just a little way beyond the apron and into the long grass. It would have been a good shot under all other conditions, but here, as Hogan knew, it could often cost a stroke.

Hogan noticed other facets of the course setup that would be factors in this Open. He realized that for the first time in any championship the regular rough, untrampled by the gallery, would retain its punitive qualities to the end of the tournament, because, for the first time, the entire Open course was properly roped. The crowd could not walk on the rough just beyond the edge of the fairway, tramp it down, and make it innocuous. The experiment of roping the fairways to keep the crowd back had been tried at Baltusrol, and it was a complete success at the Olympic Club, where more shots were seen by more people than in any previous Open. Most of us did not understand properly what this would mean until it was all over. Hogan knew before the championship began, and he knew something else that we all saw but did not judge properly. He saw that the fog-drenched fairways would cut down on the length of the tee shots, forcing the use of longer clubs for second shots to targets which the encroaching rough had made unfairly small. These shots might also be more difficult to control because of the moisture on the ball. The figures announced after the tournament bore Hogan out in quite a remarkable way.

Trent Jones, the golf-course architect who altered the Open courses for the USGA at that time, kept records throughout the tournament to give him information on which to base future alterations. These figures showed that the average length of the tee shots of the top players during four rounds on the Lake Course was a mere 216 yards. On all balls struck from the tees the average roll

was under ten yards. These figures astonished the players, who furnished them. Hogan was in no way surprised. He had adjusted immediately on his practice
rounds to the fact that accuracy on every tee shot and
fairway shot was called for and that the odds were heavily
against pulling off a gambling shot. He hardly hit one
full-blooded shot in the old Hogan manner until he felt
that he was moving safely home on Saturday afternoon.

There are no words unused in praise of Hogan's golf,
but it may be added here that he probably knew more
about the playing values of a golf course than any man
who ever lived. He knew beforehand how very difficult
the Lake Course was, and so he came into the championship with the comfortable knowledge that this would
make it easier for him to win his fifth title. It was as
though he knew from the beginning how the tournament
would develop from round to round, and how he would
be the only one of all the 162 starters who would know
what to do about it. Why, then, didn't he win? Because of
a man named Fleck, upon whom Hogan did not figure
and whose astonishing performance could never have
been forseen either by Hogan or anyone else who is not
clairvoyant. There seems no doubt whatever that Hogan
got the 72-hole score, 287, that he had figured would win
the tournament. Aside from Fleck's matching total, it was
five strokes below the next best score for the seventy-two
holes.

The first-round scores confirmed Hogan's estimate of
the Lake Course. Of the 162 starters, 82 failed to break 80.
That so many players good enough to qualify for the
Open could not break 80 is astonishing. But no matter
how difficult the conditions in any particular round of a
tournament, there always is some individual who gets a
score. Hogan, secure in his knowledge, was unperturbed
by Tommy Bolt's first-round 67. Ben was in fourth place,

five strokes behind at 72. Forty names were listed on the scoreboard above that of Jack Fleck, who was tied for 22nd with 76.

After two rounds, though, Hogan and Fleck were tied at 145, and they were only one stroke off the lead. Fleck had done a 69 in the second round and Hogan a 73. This was the first time Fleck's name had been mentioned in a news dispatch from an Open, and he was described in the New York *Herald Tribune*, I blush to say, as "an obscure municipal-course pro out of Davenport, Iowa, to whose 69 no one is attaching much importance". The *Herald Tribune* correspondent on the scene hardly gave it any attention at all, and he did not see one of Fleck's 69 strokes.

So Hogan and Fleck began the final day all even and ended it the same way. But in between the time Hogan teed off Saturday morning nearly two hours ahead of Fleck and the late afternoon when Fleck made his way home, one of the most exciting stories of a fascinating tournament developed. Hogan played another 72 in the morning, and, when the final round began, he had moved from one stroke behind the lead to one stroke in front of everybody. However, since many still were playing their third rounds when Ben began his last one, he did not know he would be in front after everyone had played 54 holes. He knew, though, that he had got the score he wanted, and he felt sure he would get an even better one in the afternoon. Fleck, of course, still was in the process of doing his third-round 75, and when he brought it in, even those who had taken notice of his halfway position now forgot him. Things were working out as Hogan had figured. The course and the tension were having their effect. Ben's 70 on the final round was doubtless just about the score he sought, a well-considered and well-executed figure which he arrived at without flourish and without strain.

Having gone out early, Ben posted his 72-hole score in mid-afternoon, and when he came to the final green he was proclaimed champion by the huge crowd gathered there. The scoreboard showed that the closest contenders had fallen away one by one during the day or were now in the process of doing so. There was little doubt that Ben Hogan had become the first man in history to win the U.S. Open five times, one more Open than Bob Jones had won. Hogan believed it, though he kept repeating, "Let's wait and see. It's not over yet." But he presented the ball with which he had holed out to Joe Dey, the Executive Director of the USGA, to be placed in Golf House. Dey came to the press room to show us the ball.

I sat down to write a lead for the Sunday paper announcing Hogan's feat. Because it now was around 7 o'clock in New York, a description of the day's play had been sent earlier and was in type waiting for me to write the lead with the final result. I dared not send a lead announcing Hogan's victory until it was an actual fact certified by the scoreboard. I gave it to the Western Union wire chief with instructions to hold it, and then I sat down to study the scoreboard. What I saw—what everyone saw—was that of all the players still on the course, Fleck was the only man who had a slight chance of catching Hogan. At Olympic, the 8th hole, a short par-3, sits right below the clubhouse, and the ninth tee is nearby. Fleck had already driven from the ninth when Hogan holed out for his 70 and 287 total, and, as Jack walked away at an angle down the ninth fairway, he heard the cheers that proclaimed the apparent champion.

Fleck had no gallery to speak of. Concerned only with Hogan, no one gave Fleck a thought. He knew what the cheering meant, though, and as he headed into the two-hour journey through the final nine holes, it is certain that he also knew what he would have to do in order to overtake Hogan. He may have dismissed it as not likely to happen, for he had to play the last nine holes in 33 strokes, two under par. On such a course and under all the pressure of a final round of an Open, such a score seemed altogether impossible to the thousands, spectators and journalists alike, gathered at the Olympic Club. Fleck, after all, was a public-course professional without experience in this kind of high-pressure golf. In his thirty-two years he had done nothing in the least out of the ordinary. Fleck, however, could play golf, and now he lifted his game to a level he had never reached before. By this time, Hogan had given his victor's interview in the locker-room still protesting cautiously that it was not over yet. By then, Fleck had played three of the last nine holes and was busy with the 13th, the 67th of the tournament. He had picked up one birdie and now needed one more, along with five pars, to tie.

I had arranged my seat in the press room alongside Francis Powers for old times' sake. Francis had been away from golf for a long time, but this week he was covering the championship for his old paper, the Chicago *Daily News*. Wise in the ways of the game and of newspapering, he said to me, "Never mind if he can or can't do it. You get the hell out there on that course and watch this fellow come home. Scoot!"

It was thirty-odd years now since I first came into the profitable habit of following this man's advice, and it was a hard habit to break. I scooted. Because he was writing for an afternoon paper two hours ahead of San Francisco, Francis had to stick where the score came in hole by hole.

I caught up with Fleck at the 14th and, with the help of a marshal, pushed my way through the crowd. Fleck stood on the tee. Playing with him was Gene Littler, who had come within one eight-foot putt of tying Ed Furgol at Baltusrol in the 1954 Open. I squatted down so those in

back could see, and I had a good look at Fleck as he waited
and then drove. He was a little above average height and
extremely slender. The impression he gave was of wiri-
ness rather than strength, and there was little about him
that would cause one to notice him. He was dressed exactly as Hogan was dressed: white shirt, dark slacks and
peaked white linen cap. But the difference in their appearance was nevertheless considerable. There wasn't a
chance that this mild-appearing man ever could have the
look in his eye that caused his fellow-professionals to call
Hogan The Hawk.

The 14th was a dangerous hole, 410 yards long with a
deep gully skirting the left side nearly the whole way. I
studied Fleck as he teed his ball and looked down the
fairway. His face wore a dreamlike expression revealing
nothing. He stood one under par now with five holes to
play. On one of them he had to get a birdie if he was to
catch Hogan. It was possible, certainly, but it seemed
more likely that he would lose a stroke or more to par.
These finishing holes had caused the greatest trouble for
the players throughout the tournament. Fleck did not appear nervous, and I wondered if he actually understood
the possibilities for glory and gold that lay ahead. He hit
a serviceable drive on the 14th. Obviously there was nothing wrong with his method. Something, nevertheless,
was wrong with his second shot, a poorly played approach. Fleck was apparently feeling the strain after all.
He wasn't able to get down in two putts for his 4, and
now he was only one under par on his last round. The 67
he needed (par was 70) depended now on his making two
birdies in the last four holes. The 15th, a par 3, and the
18th, a short par 4, presented the best opportunities.

Fleck responded nobly to the pressure on the short
15th, hitting a beautiful medium iron that appeared to be
right up against the pin. Actually, it was five feet away,

and a five-foot putt certainly is missable even in a friendly round. But Fleck did not miss and, suddenly, with the lost stroke regained so quickly, the atmosphere grew tense. We all felt it out on the course, and no doubt Hogan felt it, too, receiving reports back in the clubhouse a mile away. For the first time, I think we began to feel that Fleck, who had turned a most unlikely prospect into an entirely possible one, might really do it. He still needed to pick up a stroke. Would he dare gamble and wait for the last hole to try for it? This was one of the questions those in the crowd asked themselves as they tried to grasp what was happening. Perhaps this also was the question Fleck was asking himself. The 18th was a short par 4, and a number of birdies had been made there during the championship, but the final green, which slants down quickly from back to front, is treacherous, and many players had three-putted.

Still appearing perfectly calm, Fleck, almost in a sort of dream state, played the formidable 16th sensibly to make certain of his par-5. It is a double dogleg, 603 yards long. He hit an excellent drive that was long enough to give him a nice open second shot down the fairway, which curved fairly sharply to the left. His second, a spoon shot, finished on the left side of the fairway and gave him a good angle to the flag. His third, a solid pitch, finished on the fringe. He came close indeed to holing his thirty-foot chip for a birdie. In order to tie Hogan, Fleck would now have to birdie either the seventeenth or the eighteenth.

The 17th was the most difficult hole on the Lakeside course. It had been changed from a par 5 to a par 4 for the Open, but it still measured 461 yards. The second shot was uphill from a fairway that tilted sharply down from left to right as it climbed to a partially blind green. Fleck played a superlative second. It ran close by the pin and came to rest at the back of the green some forty feet or so away. He made a wonderful approach putt and tapped in his short putt for a par.

The whole championship came down to how well this unknown golfer played the seventy-second hole. All those who had followed Fleck now rushed to find places from where to watch the climax. Despite the thousands who had been camping on this finishing hole for hours, it was not difficult to find room. The eighteenth at the Olympic Club is one of the most dramatic finishing holes in championship golf. The green sits at the end of a natural amphitheatre with grassy slopes rising steeply behind and beside it. All the spectators can sit or stand and see all of the play from tee to green. The hole is only 337 yards long, but the drive must be made from an elevated tee down to a frighteningly narrow fairway that runs to a tightly-guarded green which slopes from front to back. It is just a drive and pitch, but all along the left there is a bank of thickly matted rough that spells instant doom.

At the top of this bank is a walk leading up to the clubhouse. It runs past the door of the press room. I climbed there now, ready for a dash if Fleck should birdie the hole and tie Hogan. He struck the drive down the left, and a groan rose from the crowd as the ball rolled a little way into the rough at the base of the bank. These were the same people who had proclaimed Hogan champion two hours earlier. Now they were yearning to acclaim this slender, courageous man who had a chance to catch the greatest golfer of his time and might, indeed, become champion himself.

There was silence as Fleck stood in the rough behind his ball. He examined his lie, measured the distance to the flag, and then took his wedge from the bag. He played the all-important pitch without dawdling. The ball rose high, a perfectly hit shot. It came to rest a little above the pin and about seven feet away.

Some had taken four putts on this slippery green that slanted from back to front. One or two had rolled the ball entirely off the green, and many had taken three putts. Very few players in this Open had gotten down in one putt on this green, even from closer positions than Fleck's. Every person in the crowd certainly knew by now what this right-to-left putt meant: a tie with Hogan and a playoff tomorrow if it went in; second place and back to the comparative obscurity of the Davenport Municipal Golf Course if it didn't. Hogan knew this, and he had come out to stand on the high ground above and watch the denouement of Fleck's melodramatic bid.

Fleck surveyed the line quickly, took a little practice swing just short of the ball as golfers do, placed the putter in front of the ball and then lifted it back. For a few seconds he stood motionless. Then he struck the ball with that fluid motion that signifies a natural putter. The ball moved to the right, and people gasped thinking it had been struck off the line. Then it took the subtle break to the left and rolled squarely into the center of the cup. He had read the green perfectly, no easy matter under all that tension. When the ball dropped, a roar went up and few louder can have been heard at an Open championship. Hogan had drawn excited applause earlier when he had walked off the home green but that now seemed comparatively mild. Fleck had upset everything that people had decided would happen, and he had proved once more that the Open is an event whose script never can be written in advance.

The next, day, Fleck defeated Hogan in the play-off, 69 to 72. It was not as exciting as the day before. Hogan never was ahead, and the result could be foreseen somewhat in advance. Fleck, who seemed once again to be playing in a trance, never stopped hitting brilliant golf shots. At the end, when he had taken the title we thought would be Hogan's, Fleck had played five rounds on this demanding course, and three of them had been under the par of 70. In the whole tournament there had been only seven rounds under 70, and Fleck had accounted for three of them. Hogan never was able to move below par, although he played one precise shot after another.

In retrospect, the tragedy of Ben Hogan was that somewhere during his four journeys around the Lake Course he didn't save the one stroke that would have made all the difference. If one short putt had dropped for him during the tournament proper, it might have made a difference in our later assessment of his career. Such is the game of golf. The unfortunate thing for him, really, is that he was not playing behind Fleck instead of in front of him. Then he would have known that he needed to save another stroke. And if he had known, is there anyone who had watched Hogan in a major event who could believe that he would have failed to pick up that stroke? I am as certain as can be that if Hogan had had any notion that the score he was compiling would not be good enough, he would have rectified that promptly. There is no doubt in my mind that he believed he had come in with the score that would make him champion once again, and that he felt the margin was quite comfortable.

I thought it would be enough, and I admit to a slight momentary gladness when it was not, an emotion unworthy of an "objective" reporter. Golf is a game that involves the emotions—personal likes and dislikes—perhaps to a greater extent than other games. It is possible for a golf reporter to hope fervently at one moment that something does not come off and then to rejoice in the wonderful story with which he has been presented when it does occur. It is for us in the end always the story above our own preference. Twice on that Saturday of fluctuating fortunes, we were caught and pulled back from the object of our hopes by the story. As Hogan moved unfalteringly toward the 70 that we thought had made him champion, I realized that I preferred him to remain tied with Jones at four Open titles each. But a little later, when I and all the others thought he had done it, we sat down with eagerness, even joy, to write of his triumph.

And then, hours later, coming home on those last agonizing holes with Fleck, I was conscious of my hope that Fleck would fail. I did not now want to see Hogan deprived of his well-earned victory. When the last putt had dropped, though the cheers of the crowd had not died, my colleagues and I were telling one another what a wonderful story it was to write. And so it was, although it was undoubtedly the deepest disappointment of Hogan's golfing life.

When Hogan returned with the British Open trophy in 1953, he was given a ticker-tape parade up Broadway, a reception before a big crowd in City Hall Park, and an official luncheon—almost an exact duplicate of the reception New York had given Bob Jones twenty-three years earlier. That evening the USGA gave a small dinner for Hogan at a New York Hotel, and Jones, who had been in Boston for treatment of his crippling ailment, came down for it. Seated at a table close below the dais, I studied the faces of the those two champions so similar in performance, so different in personality. Here, I thought, was a most striking and revealing contrast. Hogan's face, dark and handsome in a boldly rugged way, revealed great strength and determination, though his whole personality seemed softened that night, made more attractive by his appreciation of the honors done him during the day. But I thought just a touch of arrogance also remained.

Jones's face was soft, gentle and filled not only with light but with an even greater strength of another kind.

The lines were modelled, sculptured by the character that was in him and the suffering he had born. His countenance bore no resemblance to the young Bobby Jones. I searched for a trace of the features of the schoolboy friend I had known, and could find none. Hogan, too, had suffered much, but his face did not reveal the effect of it. Hogan's features, I thought, had hardly changed at all from those of the young professional I had first seen in the 1930s. Over the years they had merely grown older. The young Hogan, already strong, self-reliant and self-controlled, was easily recognizable in this strong middle-aged face. The young Jones, overly sensitive, out-going, and with weaknesses to overcome, had been transformed.

As the eating part of the evening progressed toward the inevitable speech-making, I recalled what Henry Longhurst, of the London *Sunday Times* had written of Hogan's victory at Carnoustie, an account I had read only that very day: "His final 68, 34 out, 34 in, was an exhibition as flawless almost as Bobby Jones' historic 66 in 1926 at Sunningdale." I looked up at the two of them chatting so amiably side by side, and it seemed to me that comparing these two was not only natural but inevitable and, in a sense, necessary. Although I did not know that night that Hogan's victory string also had run its course, I ran quickly through the two careers separated by time.

In the eight years between 1923 and 1930, Jones won four U.S. Open and five U.S. Amateur titles, along with three British Opens and one British Amateur. In a similar eight-year period, Hogan, in spite of his near-fatal accident, also won four U.S. Opens, two PGA Championships, two Masters, and the British Open the one year he played in it. Jones wound up his victory march with his Grand Slam. In 1953, his final year at the top, Hogan played in six tournaments. He won five, including the three biggest—the Masters and the U.S. and British Opens—by record scores on outstanding courses. There is nothing to place alongside this unless it be the Grand Slam itself.

Both of these superlative performers came to supremacy after years of frustration. Young Bobby had been good enough to win years before he broke through at Inwood in 1923. When Hogan won his first major title in 1946 after repeated failures, he was already six years older than Jones had been at retirement. One other striking parallel exists. Each began his last and most triumphant championship year in remarkably similar circumstances: on neighboring courses in the flowering Georgia springtime.

Still with the picture on the dias before me, I thought of the vivid differences that lay below these similarities. Jones was one in whom greatness was immediately apparent. Even as a schoolboy, he was able to do nearly everything he did do later. We know that he came to mastery after years of failure, but it is difficult not to think of him as springing fully equipped for the fray, so extraordinarily talented was he.

Hogan was no instant prodigy. He came from the caddie pen, and there was about him few intimations of immortality. What Jones had, what Bob was born with, Hogan had to acquire, and as I sat below them that evening thinking of these things, it came to me for the first time that in all the years I had been closely associated with Jones, I could not recall once having seen him on a practice tee. Hogan I had watched hit hundreds of practice balls on many occasions. Surely, I reflected, Jones must have practiced and I must have seen him, but I could not honestly recall a single instance. One never thought of Jones as "learning" or "practicing".

Hogan, almost from childhood, worked unceasingly to

excel, and the fierce will to do so was the force that drove him. No one ever set himself higher standards nor worked harder to reach and maintain them. The drive that was in him produced a certain impression of ruthlessness as compared with Jones's gentle graciousness. Hogan was a craftsman for whom a lifetime of endeavor was well spent in pursuit of perfection. He labored long in the humility of self-criticism to reach a peak of achievement, and he drove himself relentlessly.

Here we have their principal difference as golfers. Here is Jones, the artist, Hogan, the master craftsman. In style, there is no comparison, and no one who remembers Jones will insist that there is. Jones's swing, one might say, was done in waltz time, and merely to see it was a joy. Hogan's was not a picture swing. It was entirely functional. His hands moved swiftly with the precision and rhythm of long experience, not with the beautiful flow of Jones's. It was the seemingly inevitable result of Hogan's swing that pleased, not the swing itself. The preliminary stance gave no hint of the tremendous sequel. There was a certain beauty in Hogan's game, nevertheless, but it was the beauty of mechanical perfection, not of artistry.

How different was the way of Jones, the amateur who played for fun, and when at twenty-eight, competition no longer was fun for him, he gave it up without regret. Many cannot comprehend what Jones did. During the years that corresponded to Hogan's long period of preparation, Jones not only set his great record in the major championships but went through high school and college, earning a degree in mechanical engineering at Georgia Tech, a second B.S. at Harvard (where he read history and literature and studied languages), and, after studying at Emory Law School, an LLD. He made his living practicing law in Atlanta.

When you write of Jones, therefore, you write of a kind of limited tournament exposure no serious golfer settles for today. Any amateur of comparable skill now joins the professional tour long before reaching golfing maturity. Jones seemed to embody in himself that ideal theoretical concept of the amateur sportsman raised to its highest degree. His was, moreover, a personality entirely separable from the game at which he excelled, since he continued to grow in stature long after his exploits were in the record books.

At this point in my musings, Jones rose to speak. He rose painfully, as I knew well, if others did not. He might have remained seated, but it was an effort that he felt was due Hogan. He said his friends were reluctant to speak to him of Hogan and himself for fear of embarassing him. But it was they, he said, not he, who were embarrassed. He saw no reason not to compare Hogan and himself, although he was not in too favorable a position to do so because of his condition. Still, he had seen enough, and there was the record. It stood to reason, he thought, that the best golfers of the present day—and there were now many more of them—should be better than those of his time. Athletically speaking, everything had improved. People ran faster, jumped farther, vaulted higher.

It was the custom, Bob pointed out, to say that the best golfers of any earlier time would still be at the top, or near it, if they were playing in a later time, say, 1953. He felt there was some truth in that, but such a thought might also be turned around the other way. He would like to do just that. Suppose, he said, that Ben Hogan had been playing in the four U.S. Opens that he, Jones, had won.

I was watching Hogan closely while all this was being said, and I saw something in his face I had not seen there before. I saw that he was sincerely and deeply touched.

He had approached the occasion with a rather charming modesty, and he had made a good speech in response, one with humility in it and a certain rough eloquence.

There were many occasions with Hogan that burn in the memory, and I cannot let this man go without mentioning the last one of all.

Gay Brewer won the Masters of 1967 in an exciting head-to-head battle with Bobby Nichols. So the book says, but I would have to look it up to know the details. I need no book to tell me about Hogan's last nine holes played on the Saturday that April, a brief, intense and electrifying performance by a man now fifty-five years old, all his winning years long past. I remember every stroke, every gesture, every club used and the great drama created for an immense crowd that had accumulated as he neared the end of what we looked upon as a perfect nine holes of golf.

Hogan had come to Augusta with an ailing shoulder, left over from his near fatal accident of 1949, and with the putting troubles that had plagued him for a dozen years. He had played little in recent months, and little was expected of him beyond the intangibles his mere presence always gave to any golfing occasion. Actually, he was hitting the ball about as well as ever, and people went out of their way to see him do it, even though his first two rounds of 74-73 left him well down the list. Then it all began to come together for him one last time, as he approached the mid-point of his memorable third round. He had done the first nine in par 36, and I count it one of the most fortunate things in all my golfing life that I happened to pass just as he was moving from ninth green to tenth tee. I was on my way to pick up the leaders after getting off some stuff for the early Sunday editions, which would go to press before the winner was known. I had now to wait for the day's results before going back to the typewriter. Thus it happened that I was there on the tenth teeing ground at the top of the slope in front of Bob Jones's cabin when there came back to us for an all too brief period the Hogan of 1953.

These next four holes at Augusta, ten through thirteen, have been called by someone, whose name I wish I could remember, "the toughest stretch of golfing topography man has yet devised", and they may be the most beautiful yet devised also. Here is where many a potential Masters champion has met disaster—a stretch of terrain no golfer with a low score ever entered without nervousness and a touch of hydrophobia, for water waits insidiously everywhere. Hogan played these four holes in twelve strokes, 3-3-2-4, four birdies in a row, and when he left the 15th green, the second par-5 on the nine, he had made five birdies in six holes. Pars deliberately played at the 16th and 17th brought him to the 18th tee needing one more birdie to tie both the lowest score ever made on Augusta's back nine, 30, and his own lowest score at the Masters, 66. Off the elevated tee, he took the narrow, dangerous route close to the trees on the left, and then hit a firm 5-iron about seventeen feet above the pin.

The ball, I think, had finished about where Hogan wanted it, but for the rest of us—tens of thousands by this time—his putt seemed too long and the slope too slippery to be holed without difficulty. Our desire to have the putt go in had nothing whatever to do with the winning or losing of the Masters, for, even with his rousing dash, Hogan was out of contention. So how could it matter? Well, it did matter. It mattered so much to me that I wonder if I had, at any time, wished so hard for a putt to drop or was so tense when it was being played. I think everyone standing there felt the same. We had seen twenty-nine perfect shots in the two hours or so since we had stood with Hogan on the tenth tee, and one imperfect shot, even on a breaking, downhill putt was unacceptable. In retrospect, it was the most important shot of that whole Masters week for me, and when it slid slowly into the cup, we did not leave Hogan in doubt of how we felt.

Augusta's treacherous second nine had been played by Hogan in 30 strokes, every single one of them perfectly struck, behaving exactly as the striker wished. The two 4-wood shots to the par-5s, the 13th and 15th, were so sweetly hit that I was about to remark that they had never been equalled in Masters history. I cannot say that because Gene Sarazen hit a 4-wood into the cup on the 15th in 1935 for his celebrated double eagle that sent him into a tie with Craig Wood and then on to victory in their playoff. I did not see that Masters, and I am sure the Squire will forgive me for thinking there may have been just a little luck involved, whereas Hogan's two 4-wood shots on the back nine in his third round went exactly as he wanted and expected them to go. And he looked as if he might repeat them all day long without even a slight variation.

It always is a thrill in sports when an old master long past his best days comes back to delight us, and I do not think I have seen anything in golf more rewarding both as it occurred and in retrospect. I am grateful to what in the old days we called the gods of golf for permitting me this opportunity, and grateful to Ben Hogan for putting on this wonderful show in the twilight of both our golfing lives.

CHAPTER IX
KEN VENTURI AND THE
1964 U.S. OPEN AT
CONGRESSIONAL

A review of the Open championships I have attended leads to the conclusion that the U.S. Open of 1964, won by Ken Venturi at Congressional Country Club, in Washington, D.C., was the most exciting, the most appealing and the most rewarding to write about. It also was the last Open played in three days with a double-round on the third, so that the conditions which brought about its dramatic turn of events cannot occur again unless there is a return to the old format. I am wondering, as I prepare to relive the feelings and experiences of those torrid three days at Congressional, if there ever has been another championship as full of those elements which make the game's No. 1 event so satisfying to be part of and to report. The 1964 Open may have been the peak in this respect, more dramatic even than the defeat of Vardon and Ray by Ouimet, which I did not witness first hand but which was the catalyst that led me into golf reporting. It is, at any rate, inconceivable to me that any four-day tournament, with its one round per day, could match the concentrated intensity of the 1964 Open, and its stirring effect on the persons who were lucky enough to be there. Because I was unalterably opposed to the change in the format from three to four days—I still believe it was a mistake—I am inclined to gloat a little that this Open was the last of the old kind, and perhaps I look upon it with a perverse pleasure.

There have been any number of Opens that came to exciting climaxes between the dawn and sunset of closing Saturdays, but I never have attended another in which the plot developed steadily from the start through the unbearable heat at Congressional to focus finally on one of sport's most appealing figures triumphant at the very point of collapse. It was indeed a dramatic occasion with a strong supporting cast performing splendidly in support of a Venturi's imperishable performance.

It seemed that everything that had happened to Venturi

from the time he entered the world of competitive golf at seventeen was preparation for this moment of triumph and vindication. Venturi had grown up in the game at a time when the woods were full of talented youngsters pressing up through the amateur ranks, among them Arnold Palmer, Gene Littler, Charlie Coe, Harvie Ward, Sam Urzetta, and Billy Maxwell, all of whom were to win the U.S. Amateur championship. With them came Billy Casper, who twice won the Open; Dow Finsterwald and Bob Rosburg, who won the PGA; Gay Brewer, who won the Masters; and such able players as Tommy Jacobs and Tom Nieporte who won big tournaments on the professional tour. Venturi's father was the manager of the pro shop at the Harding Park public course in San Francisco, and the boy was introduced to golf almost as early as he could swing a club.

Four of the U.S. Amateur champions—Ward, Coe, Littler, and Urzetta—were on the Walker Cup team at Kittanssett, Massachusetts, in 1953, Hogan's great year. That is when I first saw Venturi. None of the champions were more impressive than Venturi in the 9-3 American victory. He hit long irons of a quality unsurpassed even by his friend and counselor, Byron Nelson. At Kittansett, Venturi was so attractive both as a player and a personality that I disregarded some of the other players I had to write about at the Amateur championship shortly afterwards at Oklahoma City. (Littler won it.) During Venturi's two years in the Army, which followed immediately, some of us who had been so taken with him rather lost track of him, but he swam, or rather crashed back, into view at Augusta in April 1956. Now a slender, handsome, dark-haired young man of twenty-four, Ken got to the Masters at the invitation of the tournament's previous winners. Each year they choose one deserving player not otherwise eligible for the biggest golf event of the spring.

Venturi justified their choice immediately by playing an

opening round of 66 to lead the field by a stroke. No amateur ever had scored that low, and none had won the Masters. After two rounds Ken led by four, and he started the final round on Sunday with his four-stroke lead intact. We all thought we had a story that pleased us, for there was no one who had not been taken with Ken's magnetism and those wonderful irons he was either rifling or floating to Augusta National's treacherous greens. He had outplayed one of the strongest fields of professionals that could be assembled, and he began the final round on Sunday with a huge following. He had been performing with such youthful confidence that there was a strong possibility he would become the first amateur to win the Masters.

Our story collapsed slowly through the long spring Sunday as Ken took 80 strokes, and Jackie Burke, who had been nine strokes behind at the day's start, won by a stroke at 289. We all went the whole way with Venturi, because that day's story was of failure not of success. There was no one else to follow—nobody was lighting up the skies with his scoring. At the day's end, there was no round lower than the 71 which brought victory to Burke, who was already in the clubhouse when Venturi was struggling down the final holes. We stuck with him all the way because he was missing his pars by so little, and we knew that a few well-placed shots—in fact, one reassuring birdie—could do it for him. He never could manage this, and the strokes continued to slip away. That final round was a harsh experience for Venturi, and it foreshadowed the prolonged ordeal through which he was destined to suffer through in the years that lay between that crushing Masters and the triumphant Open at Congressional.

Venturi's attitude through that long afternoon of failure at Augusta gave some indication of the fortitude with which he would sustain the greater troubles to come. He made no gestures of annoyance, and he offered no excuse for his sorry performance. He concealed his disappointment well through the presentation ceremony when Burke slipped on the champion's green coat that so nearly had been his.

It was only on arrival at the San Francisco airport the next day that, under the prodding of reporters, Ken made some indiscreet remarks that were to haunt him in his days of adversity. When things go bad, people seldom are permitted to forget past indiscretions. It was traditional at the Masters at that time for Byron Nelson to serve as the playing partner of the leader on the last round, but because of the close master-and-pupil relationship between Nelson and Venturi, Sam Snead was elected to partner Venturi on the Sunday. It was not a happy choice.

At the San Francisco airport, Venturi, having had a night to nurse his disappointment, told the press that, among other things, he had not been treated fairly at Augusta, and that this was why he had not won the Masters. These remarks drew headlines across the country, and Venturi was labelled a crybaby, a tag that stuck and which, in the end, probably helped him to grow up.

It didn't bother him immediately, though. He turned pro soon afterward, and for a while life was good. He won ten tour tournaments and a lot of money before 1960, and in 1958 he was again within a stroke of tying for the Masters when Palmer put on a charge to win his first Masters. Palmer did it to him again in 1960, finishing birdie, birdie to beat him by a stroke. Venturi had not been an especially humble man during this period of comparative success, and he did not appear to be popular with his fellow pros.

Soon after the 1960 Masters, Venturi's real troubles began, and although he finished the year fairly high on the money list, he did not win another tournament for four years. Suddenly, it seemed that something vital had gone from his game, and, in addition, various physical ailments, some of them serious, began to beset him. A pinched nerve all but paralyzed his right side, and, although treatment appeared to remove the cause, the pain persisted. He also suffered a back strain that interferred with his swing, and for a time he had what was called "walking pneumonia".

By 1962 Venturi's earnings on the tour dropped practically to zero. In 1963 he earned less than $4,000 in twenty-seven tournaments. Even when free of his various ailments, he played badly. He wasn't able to qualify for the Open in 1961, 1962, or 1963, and he earned no invitation to the Masters. Still he kept trying, sometimes a little desperately, to get his game back. He stuck with the tour, and through it all he never complained, never even spoke of his troubles as he kept on at the task of trying to regain his old form. Slowly the attitude of his tour companions, the press and public began to change. Admiring pieces began to appear in the papers, and people now said that Venturi's early bellyaching and his later arrogance had been due to his youth. Now, it was agreed, he had matured through trial and hardship.

There was general and genuine gladness when Venturi's game began to come back to him in the spring of 1964. Physically he was sound again, and those long irons were whistling toward the target as of old. He qualified for the Open easily, and in the week before that championship was played at Congressional in mid-June, he tied for third in the big-money Thunderbird tournament. Venturi came to the Open once more in a happy mood, and there was no one at Congressional who wasn't happy about his return to the championship. There probably was no one who had any thought that he would be a factor in the Open which was held on the longest course—7,053 yards—in Open history. Venturi, however, carried quite a large gallery in the opening round for a supposed non-contender. The goodwill toward him could be seen and felt. Everybody wanted him to play well, for the Venturi story had been widely publicized. He did not hit the ball impressively in that first round, but he managed to bring in a 71. That was a pleasant auspice, for it is only the very good golfers who can salvage a decent score from a poor round.

On the second day, Ken had a round of 70, par for the course. A greatly reduced crowd watched him do it. Exciting things were happening elsewhere. Venturi was not regarded as likely to play a leading role in the drama or as being one of the ones who could handle the heat that had arrived in the capitol. The weather, hot all week, had climbed into the muggy 90s on Friday. The course was proving more formidable than had been expected, partly because the USGA had followed its usual practice of transposing two short par-5s into par-4s. Many players found it impossible to reach these holes with two wood shots, although the fact of their being considered par-4s induced the effort. There were other long par-4s that were difficult to reach in two, and the greens on several of these holes presented putting problems.

Nevertheless, Palmer, the co-favorite with Jack Nicklaus, had brought in a first round of 68, although his driving was loose here and there. He took a two-stroke lead into the second round, and the well-known Palmer-created excitement began to bubble. Arnie had 69 on the second round on Friday, very good golf for anybody, but, strange to relate, he actually lost part of his following in the course of the afternoon because Tommy Jacobs, three holes ahead of Arnie and his Army, was in the process of bringing in a 64. Jacobs finished by sinking a gargantuan putt of fifty or sixty feet for his sixth birdie. Combined with twelve pars, this gave him the 36-hole lead by one stroke, 136 to Palmer's 137. The 64 also tied the record-low round in the Open that Lee Mackey had set at Merion in 1950. Bill Collins, a veteran club pro and tour player, was five strokes behind in third place at 141. Venturi was tied with Charley Sifford at 142. This was the situation at dawn on Saturday. Not long after this, I arrived at the course for breakfast. For many years there had been something that drew me to the course very early on these Saturdays when a double round was scheduled to be played. I did not know then that this was to be the last of those wearing Saturdays when the third and fourth rounds were played.

Only those few responding at dawn to duty's call were about the place, and a hush enveloped the course and the clubhouse, broken only by the soft voice of the starter calling them to the first tee and sending them on their way with a subdued "Play away, please". Off they would go in pairs, melting into the fog that always seems to invade Open courses in the early hours of the day. This would be the last anyone would see of the early starters unless one should score sensationally, for it is those farthest from the leaders who set out first on the final day. As the hours pass and the air clears, the voices become louder. Quiet turns to bustle. The starter now uses a bullhorn to call the players to their work, and the crowds arrive in a steady procession, seeking vantage points for later use. This day, more than thirty thousand spectators would be on the course.

On this early Saturday morning at Congressional, the course had spun about itself a soft cocoon of yellowish haze that promised another day of intense heat. The sun had begun to burn through the opaqueness when, soon after breakfast, I followed an unremembered pair down the first fairway. The air still was sweet to breathe. With me walked Tom Siler, formerly of Chicago, now from Knoxville, one of the very best at our craft and a longtime companion of mine in golfing and other sports adventures. We sat together at the first green, Tom and I, watching the golfers come and go, waiting for the plot to develop.

It appeared at this hour that the issue might be confined to one pair, the two leaders, Jacobs and Palmer, playing together, with Palmer favored to win his second Open because of his probable greater stamina and resistance to the sticky heat, which already was approaching the 90s. No one was really thinking of Venturi. He was six shots behind the leaders at the start of play on Saturday. Siler and I no more than glanced at him as he came toward us at the first green with Ray Floyd, his playing partner. We were waiting for Palmer and Jacobs, two pairs behind. Hitting another of those beautiful irons shots that had begun to come back to him during Friday's 70, Ken stopped his pitch about ten feet from the pin. We all hoped Ken would continue to play well, but we knew that he was not the story. Then Ken putted and something happened.

It was one of those moments which, looking back at it, stands out so clearly and so vividly that it is certain to be taken as an omen. The ball, dying as it reached the hole, stopped on the very rim and hung there. It seemed to hang interminably, ready to drop but holding back as if it had a will of its own. Venturi looked intently at it, his putter pointed forward at the end of the stroke, and then, deciding that it was not going to fall, moved up to tap it in. He had taken only a step or so when the ball finally dropped, and all the breath that we had been holding was released in that instant. It seems right to say that the ball itself decided to drop. A distinct impression of volition certainly was felt by many of the people banked around the green waiting for the leaders to come upon the scene. While the buzzing noise that follows such an incident still was echoing, Siler turned to me and said something like, "This might set him off, you know".

I thought it might too. It was easy to feel that something fateful had happened, although some will think the notion fanciful. Let them. Golf is full of caprice and whim. I decided to go some holes with Venturi and to double back later to pick up Palmer and Jacobs. The way it turned out, I never did get back to them for a long stay and saw only small chunks of their play until the comparative end of the day.

Venturi made his pars at the second, third and fifth, and he picked up birdies at the fourth and sixth. I had thought of waiting at the sixth for the others to come up because of the lusty shouts from behind, but when the vanguard of the press corps, getting the word of Venturi's start, had arrived, one learned that Palmer was hitting the ball all over the landscape and already had dropped four strokes behind Jacobs. And so, after learning that Venturi had gone on to birdie the 8th at about the same moment Palmer was taking a bogey at the 6th, we all hurried forward to pick up Ken at the 9th. Now he was ahead of Palmer and within reach of Jacobs, but there still was a long way to go and the weather had become oppressive.

The ninth hole at Congressional measures a full 600 yards or close to it. About a hundred yards short of the green, the fairway suddenly becomes a deep ravine filled with trees, bushes, and deep, tangled rough. The green could not be reached in two shots, and nobody was foolish enough to try. Everyone played his second shot as close to the ravine as he dared, and then hit as delicate a pitch as he could to a small, undulating, touchy green on which putting was a problem from any distance. Venturi had played his second with the long iron he still carried in his hand as we privileged ones inside the roped fairways came up behind him. He could be recognized far away, for he was a striking figure in his dark pants, white shirt, and white cap, and he had a distinctive walk. Many golfers do. Jackie Burke, for instance, can be identified from a considerable distance by the special way in which he swings his left arm back and forth across his body while walking. Hogan's rather stiff-legged walk was unmistakeable, and Cary Middlecoff's walk was as fidgety as his backswing. A golfer's walk is directly related to his temperament, be it sanguine or melancholic, choleric or phlegmatic.

Venturi's walk was described as splay-footed, and, although I am not quite sure what that means, it seemed to fit. He was big and tall and stood very straight, but he did not give an impression of athletic suppleness as did his handsome playing partner, Raymond Floyd. He did have a certain feeling of winsomeness about him, although there seemed to be some indecisiveness in his slightly wobbly, tentative manner of walking in contrast to the determined stride of a Palmer. The crowd had quickly increased as he approached his ball, for it was easy to cut across the holes on Congressional's first nine. Thousands had filed around both sides of the ravine to the green to watch the putting, no doubt with the idea of waiting there for the other twosomes coming up. Venturi took a wedge for his pitch, and he stopped his ball about eight feet past the pin. He holed the slippery sidehill putt for his fifth birdie in nine holes. He was out in 30, and now, from far back and with no great fanfare, he had dashed into the thick of contention. I think it was here at the ninth hole in the morning that the message began to trickle through to the galleries following the two leading pairs. Venturi could win the Open.

Most of the crowd around the ninth green had decided to wait for Palmer and Jacobs, but as Venturi came off the ninth, crossed in front of the clubhouse, and then made his way down a slope to the tenth tee—a walk of several hundred yards—a good many spectators decided to go with him, and hundreds loitering around the nearby eighteenth hole joined the procession. Venturi's appeal, which was to be irresistible before day's end, was already at work. Everyone wanted to see him win, though few thought he could last. As he stood on the tenth tee, an uninhibited fan remarked, "Look at him. The poor guy's pooped already, and there's twenty-seven holes to go."

Venturi did look pretty bad. His face was flushed. His eyes seemed hot and dry under the tip of his flat white linen cap. He kept hitting those irons dead on target, though, and they produced pars on the tenth and eleventh.

The tenth fairway at Congressional rose to a somewhat higher level than the first nine, and the course generally remained at that level until it descended to the eighteenth green. That day it seemed hotter at the higher level. Although it would have been helpful to know what was going on in the pairs behind me, this was no day for darting back and forth. Golf writers usually are in poor shape, and even walking was a burden in the humidity. On such a day, little offers of help are long remembered. I was resting for a moment trying to pick up a little strength for the trudge after Venturi up the slope of the tenth fairway—a slight rise appeared mountainous—when along came a golf cart driven by Frank Hannigan, the USGA's Assistant Executive Director. Frank picked me up and we followed the play to the sixteenth, and this undoubtedly saved me the energy I needed to be able to stay until the climax of the championship. I was not feeling too strong at the time, and neither was Venturi.

That morning, though Ken seemed to be wilting fast, he a hit perfectly gorgeous iron shot to the twelfth, a par 3 of 180-odd yards, and when the putt went down, he was six under par. Behind the twelfth green there was a big scoreboard, and Ken stopped to study it before going on to the thirteenth. It showed that Jacobs had lost a stroke at the eighth and ninth holes and that at this moment, incredible as it seemed, Venturi was actually in the lead. On occasions such as this, Bernard Darwin liked to quote an old Scottish friend of his to the effect that "It's na possible but it's a fact."

It also was a fact that the cumulative effect of heat and strain was beginning to tell on Venturi. All the way in, it was a struggle for him to hold out against what at times seemed to be the threat of possible collapse. His movements became slower and less certain. His step now and then faltered. His strength seemed to have left him, and a certain lack of decisiveness came into his play.

Meanwhile, Jacobs, with some sharp shotmaking on the second nine, had begun to get back what he had lost on the first nine. I felt I should probably be watching him, for it seemed likely that Venturi would not be able to hold on. I hesitated to leave him, though. On the seventeenth, he failed to hit a tiny putt up to the hole, and missed his par. He made another weak poke at a putt of little more than two feet on the eighteenth, and missed his par again. Despite all this stumbling, he had managed to bring in a 66. It appeared he could not see clearly now, and one wondered if he were fully conscious. He seemed on the verge of collapse when they got him into the air-conditioned locker-room. A doctor who was called confirmed this and took charge of Ken.

Half an hour later, Jacobs came in with a 70 on his morning round to lead by two strokes with 206 for fifty-four holes to Venturi's 30-36-66—208. Ken had made up four strokes, but there was considerable doubt whether he would be able to play the final round in the even fiercer heat of the afternoon. Jacobs, with a six-stroke lead now over Palmer, who had shot a 75 in the morning, appeared the likely winner.

When we came back to the clubhouse with Jacobs, we found Venturi stretched out on a locker-room bench with the doctor hovering about. Ken looked thoroughly beat, as athletes say, but he was cheerful. He said he would play, since the doctor said he might. He took a good quantity of tea but no solid food, and rested for nearly an hour after swallowing salt pills.

Stepping out of the clubhouse, the heat struck one like a blow in the face. Venturi seemed only partially restored as he went toward the first tee where sweltering people called encouragement to him. Word had got about now of the doctor and the near collapse, and there was a tide of sympathy for him. At his side was the doctor, who planned to walk the whole round, indicating that help might still be needed. Ken did not look at all well, but he continued to hit his shots confidently and got his pars easily on the early holes.

Since it seemed unlikely that Venturi, even with a doctor in attendance, could stay close to the leaders, most reporters waited at the first tee for Jacobs and Palmer. I was sure we had done the right thing when Palmer, beginning in his old spectacular way, began to close the gap between himself and the leader. Then Jacobs got into serious trouble at the par-3 second and took a 5. This thrust Palmer back into the picture, but it also brought Venturi back into a tie for the lead with Jacobs. The question now was whether to go forward and pick up Ken or remain with Palmer and Jacobs on the chance that another typical Palmer charge might be in the making. Palmer settled this quickly on the next two holes when he failed to get his par on either. Eventually we caught up to Venturi at the ninth, exactly as we had on the morning's round. The script proved to be the same.

On the tee, facing the 600-yard Ravine Hole for the second time on this scorching day, Ken had seven pars on his card and was tied with Jacobs, two holes behind, who was struggling to get back to even par. Venturi played the ninth exactly as he had five hours earlier—a long, straight drive and a whistling 1-iron that was hit so far one thought it surely would roll into the ravine and bring an end to Ken's challenge. Instead, it stopped a few yards short, and he came up to it with his wedge in his hand, just as he had done in the morning. He came up on rather wobbly legs, and the face that had been flushed now was white, a dangerous sign. There was a dreamy, indolent look about him, as though he would like to lie down and take a nap. However, there was nothing dreamy, wobbly or indolent about the next two shots, and I later thought, looking back, that they made all the difference in the outcome.

The flag was where it had been in the morning, at the back-left corner of the green. There was a bunker directly behind it, and not too far behind either. Venturi looked at the flag for a moment, and his filmy eyes cleared. He set himself nicely at the ball and swung the club. The ball, rising high above the ravine, pitched a dozen feet in front of the pin, rolled ten feet past it, and sat down about the same distance from the bunker. The putt was a shade downhill, and Venturi's line broke slightly from right to left. It was a more difficult birdie putt than the one he had made in the morning, but Ken struck it with what seemed to be complete confidence, and it was in the cup all the way. He had made another birdie on this hole where others dropped strokes, and with it Venturi was back in the lead again. I needed no urging to follow Venturi down the last nine holes, nor did others. Even Arnie's Army was deserting their general. Of course there was still the real possibility that Venturi would not make it all the way home safely. His progress on the last nine holes was painfully slow. We remembered how the strength had drained out of him on the second nine in the morning, and we feared lest something more serious happen in the afternoon. Fatigued now, he was unable to swing the club all the way through the ball and into a full finish. But it was clear by the time he reached the fifteenth that par for the round probably would be good enough, and, somehow, in spite of some weak shots, he managed to get his pars. Back behind, Jacobs was working on a 74 and Palmer on a 76. Ken was headed for a 70 and a total of 278, two strokes below the USGA's arbitrary 72-hole par but ten below Congressional's true par. Nowhere on the course was there anyone who could menace him now if only he could finish without throwing any strokes away. He knew and we all knew that he had it won if he could keep on his feet a little longer.

The eighteenth at Congressional is an unusual finishing hole, and when Venturi came to it, there occurred one of the most moving scenes in my golfing experience, and, I think, in the history of golf. This par-4 of 465 yards bends slightly to the left into a wide fairway that slopes down to a peninsular green which extends out into a pond. There is water on three sides of the green. It is a frightening sort of hole to play, and all of it could be seen by the thousands sitting or standing along the right side on the high ground between the eighteenth and tenth fairways. Since it was now known that Venturi's odessey was about to come to a successful end, just about all of the huge crowd was out there on the hillside when Venturi arrived.

Ken took a 5-iron for his second after a rather weak drive that, nevertheless, had stayed out of trouble. He let the shot fade, and the ball found a bunker on the right fifty yards or so from the pin. It didn't matter now. He had strokes to spare and was going to win. As he came slowly down the slope, stumbling a little, the people stood up as he walked past. When he was halfway down, everyone was clapping their hands and making a continuous cheering noise that amounted to an ovation. Venturi stopped for a moment, weaving a little off-balance as he did so. He took off his cap and smiled a wide smile that covered the fatigue and strain in his face. Now everybody was calling to him, shouting his name all down the hillside as he went on his shaky way, waving his cap to them. A golfing moment to remember.

Ken played a superb wedge shot from the sand ten feet from the pin and holed the putt for his par 4. He let the club drop, lifted both arms high in a gesture of relief, or thanksgiving and of gratitude, and there was on his face a glow of joyous happiness and an expression that is impossible for me to describe. The whole hillside, with its many thousands, burst into a prolonged roar that no Open has ever matched for sheer joy.

A photographer close to the green caught this picture an instant after the final putt had dropped—Venturi with an expression almost of prayer—and it will always be one of golf's most beautiful pictures for those who know the circumstances. I have kept this picture in my mind, because Venturi was again hit by adversity a few months later before he could fully savor the rewards of being the national champion. His hands went numb because of some nerve trouble that didn't respond to treatment. He never won another tournament as he went his uncomplaining way. This picture, taken at his moment of triumph, keeps fresh for me a gala day in golf and recalls the moment of a lifetime for a true champion.

CHAPTER X
THE AGE OF ARNIE

Golf historians, those chroniclers of the game's progress from the feather-stuffed leather ball through the revolutionary gutty to the high-velocity missile of today, usually sort their material into periods to which they give the name of the personality they feel most clearly represents it. Thus we have the Age of Vardon, the Age of Jones, and the Age of Hogan as a sort of mythology of the most significant periods. This is convenient for historic purposes, but the arrangement of golf history into periods named after the dominant stars is unfair, for all that. It overlooks the fact that in golf, as in the history of civilization itself, development is a constantly flowing stream. A new age begins, or at least is in progress, long before the old one ends, and such arbitrary compartmentalizing does scant justice to those who also were players of stature and persons of worth. I seriously doubt that it is ever useful to range one age against another. Things are likely to have quite a different appearance at the time they are happening compared to the neatness and completeness that the historian bestows upon them afterward.

The most representative players of a period are not always the most interesting. Byron Nelson, who won one Open in a three-way playoff in 1939 and lost another the same way in 1946, might well have given his name to an era but for the cessation of the major championships during the Second World War. It was Byron's misfortune to have his best years when we were all occupied elsewhere, or at least looking the other way. He was the best golfer of the period and the dominant figure of those pre-Hogan years. He was not for me, however, the most interesting player. That person was a slim, suave and handsome gent named Lloyd Mangrum, who came out of the war trailing glory, purple hearts and a glittering record. Immediately upon his return to the golf scene, he came through a terrific storm in the 1946 U.S. Open with three birdies on the last six holes to win the play-off at the Canterbury Golf Club, in Cleveland, from Nelson and Vic Ghezzi. Thunder, lightning and drenching rains were children's stuff compared to the tempest Lloyd had been through.

Most golf people have now forgotten how Mangrum won at Canterbury, preferring to recall how he lost another Open, the one at Merion in 1950. He was a personality who had far more fascination for me than the celebrated golfers I have watched and admired. For a little while, he was the most exciting putter imaginable, though probably not the best. I remember Mangrum easily, pleasantly and vividly, while it requires a conscious effort on my part to call up men who won twice as many titles and barrels more money. Lloyd was the epitome of the bold, insouciant, devil-may-care but shrewd gambler who'd bet you the sun wouldn't rise if the price were right. Francis Powers and I always referred to him, and even addressed him, as Gaylord Ravenal, the riverboat gambler of "Showboat". And he could play golf. Remember that round of 64 at the Masters in 1947?

The representative figures of a period are not necessarily the most significant. In the Age of Vardon, what about Francis Ouimet, whose influence on the game, many people think, was even more profound than that of the sainted Harry himself? And when you refer to the 1920s as the Age of Jones, as you must, where does that leave Walter Hagen and Gene Sarazen, two undeniably great champions?

Nevertheless, if names are to be assigned to periods, this kind of thing cannot be avoided. The Age of Hogan, for the historian, probably ended in the mid-1950s, though it lingered on because of the strong possibility that Ben might win again, and he did come close in the Open as late as 1960. Hence the reluctance to close out an age and to assign a new name to a next one. The new age, nearly always, is being born while the old one persists. The age that followed the Age of Hogan named itself. It stretched from Ben's slow decline in the late 1950s right into the 1970s. It bears the name of Arnold Palmer, and any schoolboy who reads the sports pages or turns on the living room TV box can tell you all about it. We were in the Age of Arnie, and we remained in it even after it had passed into history. That is the surprising thing. Going into the 1970s, Palmer had not won a major title in six or seven years, and several other golfers had far outstripped him in achievement. But with all the world's big titles in the hands of his rivals, with colorful new players on the national scene, and with Palmer himself known to be well past his best days, the Age of Palmer continued on, as far as the public was concerned. Everyone felt that Palmer was done as the dominant golfer, but let him get a round going and nothing else happening on the course mattered—not even fireworks by Jack Nicklaus, Lee Trevino or Gary Player. Arnie's Army mustered again, despite the fact that years earlier we had all felt that Nicklaus was forcing on us the necessity of establishing a new and super age named after him. His opponents and golf people in general were as one in declaring that Nicklaus played a new and different game that was superior to anything that had been seen before. Still the crowds would desert him quickly if Palmer showed signs of mounting a charge. The reason for this is self-evident.

The period of the 1960s was the time of the flowering of the game from the point of view of spectator participation, both actual and vicarious. It was an age of enormous purses and TV exposure. The parade of tournaments, with fabulous amounts of money distributed among mercenaries of high skill, became practically a year-long weekly show moving across the country from town to town as the old circuses of our youth had once made memorable their yearly visits to our hometowns. As the 1950s closed and the new decade began, professional golf became for its leading practitioners almost incidental to the deluge of business opportunities it offered. Soon the ubiquitous player's agent inhabited the scene, and there began a scramble among them to handle the extra-curricular interests of the stars—TV appearances; endorsements of golf equipment and other manufactured goods; instructional wisdom in syndicated columns and in books to which their names could be attached; and all manner of ventures and investments unconnected with the game.

Commerce raised its Janus-faced head, and soon it was only the marginal tour player who did not have his personal manager. Golf became largely a business, and many of the golfers played the game solely, it seemed, to make money, that age-old beacon of hope and despair. It was a time when, in fields other than golf, people were becoming world celebrities without showing a real talent for anything. Golfers were becoming millionaires. Tournament sponsors competed for the honor of giving away the most money, and American golf reached undreamed-of-proportions, heroic and dramatic heights, and heights of folly, too. It seemed to have been handed over to promoters, speculators, and agents who tended, because they were the businessmen, to overshadow in some cases the players they represented.

This situation, growing from year to year, needed and called for a representative figure. The moment produced the man. Palmer was the ideal, almost the predestined, athletic for such a time. He benefitted probably more than any other professional golfer from the conditions of the new age, and he stood as its symbol. Jack Nicklaus and Billy Casper each won the Open twice during this period, and Julius Boros added his second Open and his first PGA, a title Palmer was never able to win. During this period, Gary Player won all four major titles—the U.S. Open, the British Open twice, the Masters, and the PGA twice. Nicklaus won the British Open twice, the PGA twice, a third and then a fourth Masters. Lee Trevino, a public favorite, also had come on the scene and done amazing things. Would it not have been more logical for one of these champions to have given his name to the period?

There were a number of reasons why they did not, but the basic one is that Palmer, in the midst of all this flamboyance and despite the heavy physical and emotional pressure he was under, somehow was able to restore a sense of the ordinary man triumphing. Professional golf is by no means the most strenuous of sports, but it probably makes the most prolonged demands on a man's physical control. Palmer coped with these strains and, however much he profited personally, permitted us to see that big-time golf, despite being innundated by money, was not just money after all. He was able to do this because of qualities quite apart from the ability to hit a golf ball far and true. The secret of Palmer's huge appeal was that nearly everyone of the thousands who joined his army down through the years established a personal relationship with him, or felt that he had. Each had his own personal Palmer stories to tell and retell.

Other professional golfers have had a better golf swing than Palmer's, some have been more graceful technicians, but none has had what Arnie has: the human spark that glows. With his refreshing spontaneity, he appealed immediately to all of us who are lured by happy experiences in golf or haunted by unfulfilled dreams of glory. The exciting players in any game are those who involve the spectator emotionally. Some of the other winners of titles in Palmer's time achieved a nearly perfect artistry as strikers of the ball, but people tended to consult their pro-

grams when they went by. We applauded them gener-
ously when their putts dropped and stood politely aside
when they moved to the next tee. There seldom seemed
to be anything about them relating to the joy of life even
when, as occasionally happened, they assumed the role of
clowning extrovert. Sound in their shotmaking and pleasant in personality, they lacked Palmer's lustre.

No popular athlete ever looked more right for his role
than Arnie. His movements told of the character within
him. Boyish in spirit, he set the imagination afire. When
he began to move down the second nine of a round with
one of his almost irresistible charges, his galleries responded with spontaneous whoops and shouts from male
and female alike, from veteran golfers and kids, and from
people who weren't interested in golf but who had gone
out to see this man they had heard so much about. That's
how it was in the Age of Palmer.

Amid the shrill yells of "Go, Arnie" and the rumbling
chorus of approval, he achieved a rapport with golf galleries that may never have been matched in this game. He
talked to them, they talked to him, and, when they could
get close enough, they'd slap him affectionately on the
butt with rolled-up programs. The seriousness of a situation never reduced him to taciturnity. He kept on talking
to his galleries, they answered him, and he induced the
placid elements of the crowd to emerge from private to
public communication. Enlisting in Arnie's Army was like
becoming a member of an audience participation show.

There was, for instance, the nice, motherly, middle-
aged lady standing in the immense crowd around the
sixth green at Bellerive during the second round of the
1965 Open. Palmer was struggling desperately to make
the 36-hole cut. He had just put his tee-shot on this difficult par 3 over water close to the pin, and it brought a
roar that could be heard halfway to downtown St. Louis.

His first birdie of the day seemed certain. Then Palmer missed the putt, and the suffering lady's grief exploded into speech, "Oh, Arnold! Honestly!" she exclaimed, and the cry echoed in the hearts of all of us there and millions elsewhere. Yes, Arnold, honestly, how could you do this to us?

There are many instances of this wonderful relationship of Palmer with his people. We suffered for him that he might fail, and we were filled with tumultuous joy when he retrieved a hopeless situation. He seemed to be playing for us, not merely for the big check at the end. We longed for him to win, and he was the only one of his time who made us forget the huge sums for which they were competing.

The Age of Palmer was foreshadowed for some of us on a September day in 1954 when Hogan, having had his best year ever in 1953, was still golf's dominant figure. This incident took place in a corner of the locker-room at the Country Club of Detroit the day before the U.S. Amateur championship was to start. There we found Palmer, who had recently finished a hitch in the Coast Guard and was on the verge of turning twenty-four. He had not won anything important, and few of the golf writers knew him. Charlie Bartlett, of the Chicago *Tribune*, who had met Palmer when covering college golf, was asking the young man what he thought of his chances in the Amateur. Charlie never forgot the reply, and I am sure I never will either. "I want to win this one so bad I can taste it," Palmer said, and he said it with the vehemence with which a starving man might speak of food. And he did win it. Escaping narrowly from defeat in round after round until he had beaten Bob Sweeny, a former British Amateur champion, on the final green in the final round, Palmer made that match-play tournament one of the most exciting in a long while. Those comparatively small

crowds were the foundation of Arnie's Army, the first
volunteers of the horde that in future years would swarm
in frantic haste over the fairways of the land.

Palmer had that rare something, the ability to take hold
of an occasion and lift it from the flat plains of the com-
monplace. The week was no more than half over before
just about every person on the course, unless related to
some other contestant, was pulling for Arnie to win the
title. And there in the locker-room before the tournament
began, he stirred the same warm feeling of affection that
we all had for Ouimet and Jones in the faraway days of
our youth.

That was the year when Snead had beaten Hogan in a
playoff for the Masters title, and their head-to-head meeting, which caught the attention of the nation, was to be
followed by the even more memorable performance by
Hogan at Olympic Club in 1955. The new age actually
began in 1958 when Palmer won his first of four Masters.
Golf historians probably will state that the Age of Palmer
reached its summit at the 1960 Open at Cherry Hills, in
Denver. This event was preceded and followed that year
by moments so typical of Palmer and his time that they
bear recalling.

In April, 1960, Palmer came to the last three holes of the
Masters needing two birdies to beat Ken Venturi, already
in with a total of 283. Arnie was in that state his Army
called "charged up". On the dangerous 16th hole, a par-3
over water to an undulating green, Palmer's ball lay a long
way from the cup, and the putt was both slightly downhill and slightly sidehill. The ball could not be hit with
enough force to hold it on the line, for it might then go so
far past the cup as to make the loss of a stroke almost
certain. As Palmer looked the situation over, his Army
seemed reconciled to a par and got set to dash for position
on the 17th. Palmer gestured to the caddy to leave the

stick in the cup, and then he hit the ball such a whack it seemed likely to run entirely off the green, placing victory beyond reach. But it did not go past. It struck the stick squarely and finished close by. He tapped it in for his par.

Joining the troops accompanying Palmer home that day was Art Wall, a charming and talented man, who also had produced heroics at Augusta and would have been defending champion this day but for an injury. Wall was standing in the crowd by the sixteenth green when a friend told him that Palmer had intended to hit the stick and had aimed deliberately for it, since that offered the only way of getting down for a birdie 2 from where he lay. Art disagreed. He thought that this was too dangerous a tactic with two holes still left in which to get the two birdies he needed. Walking down the 17th fairway a little later following Palmer's drive, Wall said quietly, "You know, I believe you're right about the sixteenth. Going for the pin—that's just like Arnie."

Just like Arnie and like nobody else. And how like him again on the seventeenth green. He still needed a birdie to tie Venturi. To do it, he had to get down a dangerous putt some twenty-seven feet long. He struck it so boldly that it seemed it had to go into the hole. When it did, it evoked that crescendo, that special deafening roar from the Army that accompanied a bid by Palmer for a critical birdie. When the ball fell into the cup, a virtual explosion ensued. And when Arnold went on to birdie the eighteenth and win the tournament, it seemed as inevitable as fate.

Another memorable chapter in Palmer's career took place in Denver two months later. A little after noon on the final day of the U.S. Open at Cherry Hills, we find Palmer sitting at a table in the clubhouse eating a hurried lunch before starting his final round. He had played a 72 on his morning round, and he was now studying the huge scoreboard through a picture window. It showed him seven strokes behind the 54-hole leader, Mike Souchak, who stood at 208. Musing as he munched, Palmer said half to himself: "Gee, I wonder what a 65 would do this afternoon?"

"Nothing for you," a friend from Pittsburgh, Bob Drum, replied. "Forget it. You're done."

"Like hell I am," Palmer exclaimed, bristling. "Let me drive that first green, and you'll see if I'm done."

The record books show what occurred, but no book can describe the scene that unfolded in the last round of that wildest of Opens. With a ball belted so hard that it tore the thin air apart, Palmer did drive the first green 346 yards from the tee, and with this blow he was off on an incredible run of six birdies in seven holes, setting the stage for confusion's masterpiece. No such stretch of sub-par golf had ever been seen in the Open. Palmer now was very much in contention. So were about a dozen others during the next four hours of that hot afternoon when, in those days of primitive scoreboards, it was impossible at times to find out which challengers were still coming on and which were falling back. Finally through a mass of confusion came Palmer to settle matters. After he had made the turn in 30, he played the second nine errorlessly, posted a record low Open final round of 65, and won the championship by two strokes.

After studying that chaotic last round, the historian who takes note of the flow of golf from age to age will have two other things to record. First, the Age of Hogan, already embalmed and laid to rest, threatened late in the day to leave the grave in resurrection. Ben actually came within sight of a fifth Open title after he had reached each of the first thirty-four greens in the proper stroke. On the 548-yard 71st, he went in the true champion's way for the birdie that would make him champion again. He hit a little wedge pitch over a touchy water hazard straight at the pin. The ball landed on the front edge of the green. However, instead of heading for the hole, the backspin on the ball caused it to hop back into the water hazard. Ben took off a shoe and a sock, stepped into the water and played out nicely, but the damage had been done. Then, all at once, it seemed, fatigue drained the strength from his battered 47-year-old body. You could almost see the energy slipping away, and a terrible tiredness taking its place. Hogan finished with a six and a seven to end up four strokes behind Palmer's winning total of 280. It is easy to see how much the birdie-par finish, which was within his reach, would have meant to him. It would have given Hogan a record fifth U.S. Open championship.

The other thing to note, now that Nicklaus has given *his* name to a new era, is that the precocious young man finished second to Palmer with the lowest four-round total, 282, ever recorded by an amateur in the Open. And, in a nice sentimental touch for historians, Nicklaus, in and out of the lead that furious afternoon, played the final round as Hogan's partner, just as Bobby Jones, in his first Open, at Inverness in 1920 had played with Harry Vardon, that other champion whose name was given to a golfing age.

The day after these occurrences, Palmer was flying over the Atlantic on his way to the centenary British Open at St. Andrews, where he captured the hearts of the Scots as no invader since Jones, although he fell one stroke short of catching Kel Nagle after another characteristic "charge" down the stretch. This one, too, might have succeeded if the last round had not been washed out and postponed at a time when Arnie was definitely on the move. At that moment, nothing seemed beyond him. Whenever he played, it appeared likely to almost everyone that he would win, for he seemed to be destiny's darling. He would go for the bold shot with every confidence of bringing it off. He expected every putt to drop, no matter how long and winding it was, and when it did, those who watched felt that skill and not luck had brought this about.

This was the Palmer the people loved and they have continued to love him, although his star never shone so brightly as in that wonderful year of 1960 when he had just turned thirty, even though later on he won the British Open in 1961 and 1962, added two more Masters in 1962 and 1964, and on three occasions—1962, 1963, and 1966— tied for the U.S. Open only to lose in a playoff. In the later years of his reign, Palmer was rather badly overshadowed statistically by his leading rivals, but he had by then attained a mythical presence in which he no longer *had* to win to remain the world's most popular golfer. He still stirred the crowds as no other sports hero did, although by then he was playing many risky shots under pressure in an effort to stay in the fight. Even his final-round collapse—there is hardly any other word for it—in the Open at the Olympic Club in 1966 could not dampen the ardor of his admirers. With a second Open title apparently all wrapped up, he let Billy Casper pick up seven strokes in the last nine holes, and he then lost the playoff. Of course, it was not really given away, since Casper scored a 32 on the crucial nine against Palmer's 39.

It was only when time began to set in perspective the period from the end of the Age of Hogan to the 1970s that we could see how beneficial Palmer's influence had been to golf. Whatever others may have done or won, the game was fortunate that Palmer was there in a time of excessive exploitation when money alone seemed to rule. Too many golfers in these big-money days play as if they would be pleased just to finish well up in the money, and, worse still, they *are* mightily pleased when they do. As an over-forty multi-millionaire, Palmer still played for first place as eagerly as the boy in the locker-room at the Country Club of Detroit.

When he came into the press room at Augusta after winning his fourth Masters in 1964, Palmer sat for a moment or so on the raised platform silently looking out over the packed crowd of reporters waiting to question him. His lips twitched a little from inner mirth, and his face had the look of a mischievious small boy.

"A lot of you fellows out there thought I was all washed up," he said in mock scorn.

Many of us did think so. Wrong then, we still were wrong nine years later in 1973 when he was the subject of an hour-long television documentary, although he had won nothing big in the meantime. So long as he would play tournaments, Palmer never would be washed up, for there is something there beyond the winning of golf titles. Golf in our time has become a spectacle of vast importance and vast financial returns, but it still is a game played by individuals. And in his time the individual par excellence was Arnold Palmer.

Yeah Arnie!

CHAPTER XI
DOWN THE YEARS WITH
JACK NICKLAUS

In writing of Palmer as the outstanding personality of the 1960s, I am fully aware that Jack Nicklaus was and is the outstanding golfer in the world today and, because of my regard for Nicklaus as a person and golfer, I have a slightly guilty feeling about not sounding as enthusiastic about his talents as I feel I should. Entering the year 1981, Jack had won the U.S. Amateur twice, the U.S. Open four times, the British Open three times, the Masters five times, and the PGA five times. There was every indication that he would assemble the most remarkable record of all time.

Bob Jones once said that Nicklaus played a game that he, Jones, was not familiar with. It really seemed true at times that Nicklaus played a different game, one that no one before him had played, and, in this respect, he may be considered unique, since this had not been said of any golfer who preceded him with the possible exception of Harry Vardon. Awesome is the word some have applied to his game, and there have been days when the word did not seem misused. But because he had managed all his deeds without ever becoming a national hero in the sense of a Ouimet, a Jones or a Palmer, some people did not seem to regard him as highly as they should have.

I place Nicklaus high among the sports personalities I have known, but I do not really quite know what to say about him. He is not as easy to write about as the other great ones, and there is an added difficulty about a player so obviously in full possession of his powers who very likely will continue to win the big ones in the years ahead.

I watched Nicklaus develop from a husky, close-cropped tow-headed schoolboy, and I have found him over the years one of the most personable and intelligent athletes it has been my privilege to know—a thoroughly nice, unusually articulate, and kindly young man. I believe from things I have heard Nicklaus say about his own game and those of his rivals, and from what has been reported to me by others closer to him, that he understands the mechanics of hitting a golf ball better than any contemporary of his except Hogan. I have heard him say seemingly casual things about his technique and others' that struck me by their shrewdness. Most of us had missed these things. Although he is more a hitter than a swinger, Nicklaus seems to understand better than anyone since Hogan the subtleties of the golf swing. He is not just a slugger who is lost if he cannot hit the ball a mile. He has shown that he can adjust his game to a wide variety of conditions. There are certain words that fit him better than any other golfer. For starters, there is an *immensity* about his game.

Nicklaus has been kind, considerate and friendly to me on every occasion on which I have encountered him. Moreover, in his awesome procession through the golfing scene, he has given me some of the best golf stories to write. I am grateful to him for that, for as a reporter I owe him much. He cannot do to you what Palmer, Hogan, Hagen, or Jones did, but there is a very good likelihood that he can score better than any man who ever played golf.

From a writing point of view, I feel that I have treated far lesser men better than they deserved while treating Jack Nicklaus less well. His exploits made news and were good stories to write, but I feel that something was lacking in my accounts of his play. I have long pondered the reason for this and have not found an answer. It would not be right to place Nicklaus in that category of athletes who, though they win in commanding fashion, leave people comparatively untouched. There have been occasions, though, when people did not care for Nicklaus, I among them. I suspect that this may have been caused by the fact that he came along at the very height of Palmer's popularity and, like the other golfers, was relegated to being just part of the scenery. While outdoing the darling of the crowds and even beating him in direct combat, Nicklaus may have been forced to stand overly long in the deep shadow cast by Palmer. It certainly was true that Nicklaus, as a defending champion, could cause no such commotion as Palmer, who, even after he had won no major event in years, could generate a storm of applause merely by appearing on the first tee.

I first encountered Nicklaus, then a schoolboy golfer, at the Country Club of Virginia in 1955 when Charlie Nicklaus, that friendly and personable pharmacist from Columbus, Ohio, took his precocious son to the U.S. Amateur championship in Richmond. It was a fortunate circumstance for me that Nicklaus's first opponent there was Bob Gardner, the Metropolitan District's best golfer, on whom I was required to keep an eye. This was the twenty-fifth anniversary of the Grand Slam, and Bob Jones had come up from Atlanta for the occasion. It was a tournament I remember more for that than for seeing an upcoming superstar or watching the delightful Harvie Ward, one of my all-time favorites, win the title. Jones was encountered many times that week on the course in his cart. I believe it was the last USGA championship he attended. I went out at the start of the championship to see Gardner play a few holes, and I found Jones waiting to see Nicklaus. It would be nice if I could report that I knew exactly what I was looking at when I first saw Nicklaus play, because he was only a little younger than Jones had been when I first saw Bob. Actually, I probably wouldn't have remembered watching Jack in 1955 at all clearly but for the fact of connecting him with Jones.

I had to stay a longer time with Nicklaus that day than I had intended to, because of my fear that he might beat Gardner. He very nearly did, too, taking his man to the final hole all even, losing the hole and the match with a tee shot that was pulled but probably smashed farther than any other 15-year-old in the land could have smashed it. That a boy in his first championship should have done something like that no doubt should have indicated to me what lay ahead. Nicklaus was only one of a dozen or more young players one wanted to watch. The course was littered with them that first day—Joe Campbell, Johnny Pott, Doug Sanders, Joe Conrad, Rex Baxter, Hillman Robbins, Billy Joe Patton, Edwin Vare (Glenna Collett's boy)—and there were in the draw nine or ten players who had won or would win their own or foreign national titles.

Nicklaus grew steadily in the next few years. He played in seven national amateur championships, winning two of them, the first at the Broadmoor in Colorado Springs in 1959, when he was nineteen, the second at Pebble Beach Golf Links on the Monterey Peninsula in 1961. In the memorable Open championship at Cherry Hills in Denver, in 1960, he was the runner-up to Palmer at the age of twenty. I remember going out to some spot along the trail on that chaotic final afternoon to pick up Hogan and Nicklaus, who were paired. (I was a good deal more excited that Jack might win as an amateur than I was later when he did win as a professional.) Nicklaus kept his name in the sports-page headlines by his spectacular play in the Eisenhower Cup match at Merion in the fall of 1960. He turned pro at the beginning of 1962, a time when Palmer was winning tournaments all over the country with his dashing heroics. That year Arnie won four of five successive tour tournaments, all in a dazzling manner and most of them on television. He carried off his third Masters and his second British Open that year, but he did not win the U.S. Open.

Nicklaus did. It was his first tournament victory as a

professional, and he earned it by beating Palmer in a hard-fought playoff. Nicklaus now seemed set on surpassing all the standing golf achievements. He fixed his sights on the Masters record that Hogan had set in 1953 and on the Open record Hogan had set in 1948. The British Open was also clearly in his sights. Anyone who has been around sports for even a short time knows that records fall sooner or later, and those of Nicklaus no doubt also will be surpassed in their turn. Hogan's fourteen-under-par 274 in the 1953 Masters had been regarded as perfection when Nicklaus came to Augusta for the seventh time in 1965 and bettered it with a total of 271. This was a feat that Bob Jones characterized at the presentation ceremony as "the greatest tournament performance in golfing history."

I have become a little wary of presentation ceremony oratory, but I shrink from disagreeing with Jones on any of his golf judgments. Even so, the breaking of the Hogan record did not seem to me as exciting as the making of it. The reason for this may be in the character of the two men. Nicklaus is an altogether more appealing personality, but he doesn't have that something that Hogan had, the ability to invest an occasion with suspense. I think of Hogan's 274 as a nearly flawless performance over four days of play. By going over the scorecard carefully, I could no doubt find a stroke or two that did not behave exactly as he had intended, but I would have to look hard. Nicklaus's play in 1965 left an impression of wonderful driving and inspired chipping and putting—especially on the short holes where he picked up seven strokes on par—and some quite amazing recovery shots. Hogan, as far as I could recollect, had no recovery shots to make. Each had come up with a third round that put their pursuers to flight—Hogan had a 66, Nicklaus a 64. Playing conditions were ideal for both all four days, the only two of the thirty-four Masters played through 1970 for which perfect conditions prevailed.

The difference lies in the word "flawless", which everyone applied to Hogan's play. Nicklaus's play, only relatively flawed at that, contained a few comparatively poor shots which were more than compensated for by his brilliance elsewhere. On Thursday, Jack began with a sweeping hook and pulled several irons off-line. On Friday, he ran into a poor patch of golf in the "loop", eleven through thirteen. Even during his 64 on Saturday—a really terrific round of golf—there was one moment near the start when things looked bad. If it had come toward the end when the 64 was all but on the board, it would have provided an intensely dramatic moment. But it came on the second hole before there was any knowledge of what lay ahead.

As most followers of tournament golf know, the second at Augusta is a par-5 which, if the drive catches the downslope that begins two hundred fifty yards or so from the tee, can become a real birdie hole. I was standing near this point looking back as Nicklaus drove. Jack later called it a "pushed" shot, but as the ball approached at mile-a-minute speed, it had more the look of a horrendous slice. The ball was headed for the tall timber to the right with momentum enough to take it all the way to Atlanta if nothing got in its way. The growth of pine is thick there, and so, too, are the spectators, for this pleasant grove is a favorite connecting way that gives access to the second, third and fourth holes. Sometimes one strolls back and forth through the grove. At other times, a pace closer to rushing is necessary.

Nicklaus's ball rattled among the treetops in this stand of tall pines. Finally spent, it fell straight down, narrowly missing the wide-opened mouths of upturned faces. I can still hear the hollow sounds it made striking the high limbs. I dwell on this shot, only one among the sixty-four

Nicklaus played that day, because of its bearing on the record. The chances of that ball coming to rest in a favorable spot for a second shot were, I'd say, about a thousand to one. It did come to rest on firm ground in a sea of pine needles among small flowering shrubs that are planted everywhere beneath Augusta's tall trees. That alone is remarkable enough, but, from where the ball lay, the green, more than three hundred yards distant and downhill all the way, could be clearly seen through a narrow but negotiable alley. Nowhere else in that little stretch of woodland was there such an opening. A few feet this way or that, and I do not see how Nicklaus could have got out without the sacrifice of a couple of strokes. We have all, to our sorrow, been in the woods, and we know well that he, even as we, might easily have made his situation worse by hitting a tree trunk or a limb and caroming off into perdition.

What actually happened was that Jack, after a look at his lie, a heavy sigh, and a really infectious grin, seemingly in apology for his undeserved good fortune, took a 3-iron and whacked the ball so hard and so straight and so low that it ran like a jackrabbit far down the slope to within thirty or forty yards of the green. This was a tremendous golf shot, and I wonder who among us has seen a greater one? Then Jack chipped a bit beyond the pin and ran the putt down for a birdie 4 instead of the double or triple bogey he appeared to be heading for. A very lucky break? Why, yes, it certainly was, but it was luck well-earned by his circumspection before and after. An opportunity had been seized by a great competitor en route to one of the most celebrated rounds ever played in the Masters.

There were no other adventures. It was a rare and wonderful round, otherwise impeccable, with eight birdies and ten pars. It could not be faulted, but those who cherish Hogan's score above Nicklaus's, think not in terms of one 18-hole round but of four successive rounds near to perfection on each of the four days. There were no intervals in which bad shots were followed by brilliant recoveries. Jack's final round on Sunday was a triumphant march with a huge crowd, now wholly on his side, in attendance the whole way. His five-stroke lead at the start increased to nine, his 72-hole record score to three lower than Hogan's 274, and his cup to overflowing. The crowd gave him his due warmly. If they were not ecstatic, they were pleased that he had done it and given them the chance to brag at having been present on an historic occasion. Palmer had been too far back all day to matter, and at the end he was tied for second with Gary Player at 280, a score that would have won all but eight of the thirty-six Masters played through 1972 and tied seven others.

Another record performance by Nicklaus, which battered another mark by Hogan, came in the U.S. Open at Baltustrol in 1967. It may have been because I had no early deadline—in fact, no deadline at all—that I was less alert on that occasion and less aware of an impending record. My recollection of that Open was of broiling hot, humid weather, a beautifully-conditioned golf course, and a head-to-head battle down the stretch in which my sympathies were with the loser but were captured at the end of the day by the winner.

According to the USGA's strictly-adhered-to numerical pairings, Nicklaus and Arnold Palmer were playing partners for both the last two rounds. Arnold led Jack by one stroke on Saturday, and at Sunday's start both were tied with Billy Casper at 210, one stroke behind the leader, Marty Fleckman, a Texas amateur, who had also led after the first round. Usually when a record is in the making, the man who is going to make it ignites some fireworks

along the way, but Nicklaus had done nothing sensational
on the first three rounds. Accordingly, when the possibility of a record performance loomed late on Sunday afternoon, it caught many people by surprise.

On the last two days, the Metropolitan Division of Arnie's Army was out in force, noisy and highly partisan to
the point of unfairness. For the first and only time since
this boisterous organization had come into existence years
earlier, I was a buck private in the ranks, and this was a
new and strange experience. I had felt a little uncomfort-
able on my visits to the press tent with nothing to do, and
for that reason I think I was on the course nearly the
whole time, mingling with the thousands who had paid to
get in. During the last two days, I kept thinking back to
Inwood in 1923 when, at my first Open as a psuedo-re-
porter, I had been too shy to frequent press headquarters.
Now the clock had come full cycle, for I felt too useless to
be there during what proved to be my last Open. For the
first time since I had wandered innocently about Minne
kahda in 1916, when Chick Evans had won, I was, during
these days, just a spectator at an Open championship
with no duty to perform and no obligation to be detached
and non-partisan. I was not detached at all and hardly
non-partisan. I wanted Palmer to win, and I found myself, as the saying goes, pulling for him as part of the
Palmer mob on which I had formerly looked with some
amusement. I wanted Arnie to win because he had failed
to badly the year before at the Olympic Club where he
had lost in a playoff to Bill Casper. But all of us in the
Army heaving together couldn't pull Arnie Baby through,
although we indulged in some unfair practices. The Army
was dreadfully callous at times, calling to Nicklaus to hit
the ball into horrid places and occasionally even holding
up signs to indicate just where the most trouble lay. I

experienced a reaction to these tactics that surprised me. I deplored them, of course, but with a mildness that I felt ashamed of.

Nothing could have gotten Arnie through that last day, however. When Nicklaus was off to a shaky start, which was greeted joyously by the Army, Palmer moved ahead after two holes. He was tied by Nicklaus's birdie at the third, and from there on Jack was off on one of the most memorable fourth rounds in Open history, a 65 that gave him a winning margin of four strokes. A second birdie, at the fourth hole, put Nicklaus in the lead in the championship for the first time in four days.

Hours later, when he brought a four-stroke lead to the final hole, a 542-yard par 5 with trouble on the right and left all the way to the hilltop green, Nicklaus had the championship wrapped up. He was well aware that if he could finish with a birdie, he would break the old four-round record total in the Open that Hogan had set in 1948 at Riviera. This knowledge seemed to bother him a little, for he took a one-iron instead of a driver from the elevated eighteenth tee and pushed the ball into the rough and up against a TV cable. He was given a free lift. He was still in the rough, though, and he then flubbed his 8-iron recovery, moving the ball no more than forty yards or so down the fairway. This had the look of a very jittery shot, and it also seemed to have placed the record beyond his reach. Nicklaus then hit the best iron shot I have seen in such circumstances. I am mighty glad I was there to see it, because I will continue to see it in my mind forever.

Nicklaus says the ball lay 230 yards from the green, every yard of it carry, with severe problems if you were short. I would have called it a bit longer. Whatever the distance, it was enough to cause amazement when he took out his one-iron again. Bunkers to the front and left of the high green, heavy rough if you landed the ball short and tried to run it onto a green that sloped to the right. For this shot a one-iron? Nicklaus says in his book, "The Greatest Game of All", that he doubts he ever hit a better iron. With the exception of Jones at Inwood in 1923 and Hogan at Merion in 1950, I wonder if anyone has hit as awesome a long iron to the seventy-second green in our national Open championship. Peeling in from the left, the ball cleared all the trouble and rolled to within eighteen or twenty feet of the cup. Nicklaus walked up the slope to the green to the loudest applause for himself he had ever heard. He knew not only that he had his second Open title securely in his pocket but also that he had a chance to break Hogan's Open record of 276, set at Riviera in 1948. He had to hole his twenty-foot birdie putt to do so. The thousands who had rushed up the eighteenth fairway, including the members of Arnie's Army, were hoping to see Nicklaus make that momentous putt. It took him some time to collect his concentration and study the line. At length, he got set over the ball and ran it into the middle of the cup.

This time I could not say that the breaking of Hogan's record was less exciting than the making of it. Playing superbly on a course that demanded long and accurate driving, patience and judgment on the approach shots to the smallish greens, and a nerveless putting touch, Nicklaus had won me over completely. For the first time since I had seen him in the Amateur at Richmond twelve years earlier, I was a thorough-going Nicklaus fan. I regretted that it was now a few weeks too late for me to sit down at my typewriter and wrap his exploits up in sports-page superlatives.

The End

Afterword
by
Carol McCue

The end of Al Laney's wonderful book came abruptly and I wasn't ready for it. Reading his recollections brought back so many vivid memories of the players he covered, the long lunches with him in New York after he retired, the correspondence we exchanged about everything from Joe Venuti to Ken Venturi. "Following the Leaders" is the kind of book you re-read, and I'll remember forever the sharp vignettes. The players jump right off the page and back on the great courses, and their battles down the stretch are exciting and vivid.

The dictionary says an afterword is what someone says "in addition to" and/or something that "reassembles the characters", so, according to Webster, I can add a few comments of my own about Al and his "splendid companions". I was fortunate enough to know many of them. For example, I remember watching Sam Snead give a lesson to Patty Berg and listening to their discussion of the importance of "swinging to the finish and holding it", a movement they both believed enabled them to win more championships than anyone had done before. I loved hearing Gene Sarazen talk about his experiences when he started to caddy regularly when he was eight. That would be against the child labor laws today, but it got Gene started on his exciting career. I'd love to go to a Broadway musical based on Sarazen's life. Can't you just see all those tough little boys dancing and singing in the caddie yard!

Al Laney grew up in Pensacola just before the turn of the century. After the First World War, he wound up in the Paris of romance, the Paris of F. Scott Fitzgerald, Ernest Hemingway, Ford Madox Ford, Ezra Pound, Gertrude Stein, Josephine Baker, Maurice Chevalier, and the Gerald Murphys—all those talented and glamorous literary people we envied before we realized that sometimes their world fell in on them while we somehow managed to plod on with our own lives. (The Gerald Murphys—his family owned Mark Cross, the elegant Fifth Avenue store—realized how shattering the high life can be, and they came to the conclusion that 'Living well is the best revenge.' That phrase became the title of the memorable biography of the Murphys that Calvin Tompkins wrote.)

When Al arrived in Paris in 1924 and found a job with the Paris Herald, *the people on that newspaper became the new kids on the block. He commuted from their world to the world of international sport, golf and tennis principally. My knowledge of tennis comes strictly from the sports pages. However, my knowledge of golf is extensive and deep. No one has written of that world more eloquently than Al Laney. I go back to those days when the golf writers in the tournament press tents had to bang out their copy at tremendous speed in order to make their deadlines. They whipped their copy over to the Western Union telegraphers who sent it clicking at high speed to the sports desks of distant newspapers. In some ways this was a far more exciting milieu than today's press tents where the writers simply phone their stories in or use word processors.*

One of the great pleasures of reading Al's book is discovering the inner workings of the minds and sense of the great players when they faced the challenges of the big championships. He is very discerning when he describes the approaches to the game of Hogan and Jones, two altogether different men. He is no less impressive when he is discussing the unorthodox techniques of Lee Trevino and Chi Chi Rodriguez, two immense talents who have commanded our respect in recent decades. He is fascinated by the top women players. He quotes Bobby Jones saying of Joyce Wethered after a round with her in 1930, "She didn't miss one shot. She didn't even half-miss one shot, and, when we had finished, I could not help saying that I had never played with anyone, man or woman, amateur or professional, who made me feel so totally outclassed. I have no hesitancy in saying she is the best golfer I have ever seen." This brings to mind Jones's saying of Jack Nicklaus many years later after Jack had won the 1965 Masters with four stupefying rounds of power golf: "He is playing an entirely different game—a game I am not even familiar with."

Al writes that Harry Vardon, the winner of a record six British Opens between 1896 and 1914, may have been the finest golfer of all time, but after reading his explorations of the persona and swings of Hogan, Nicklaus, and other great champions, the reader is lead to believe that Bobby Jones was not only Laney's favorite player but probably his favorite person among the champions he knew, for he writes of him with such respect, compassion, and love. I saw Jones play during the Hale America at Ridgemoor Country Club, in Chicago, in 1942. The Hale America was the only national championship that war year. Many of Hogan's admirers used to speak of it as his fifth Open victory. For me, the Hale America was an opportunity to watch Bobby Jones. Jones finished far down the list, but for me he was certainly the chief attraction, wonderful to watch on the course, handsome in his major's uniform as he chatted warmly with old friends in the clubhouse before and after his rounds.

Al's descriptions of the beauty of Augusta National, Jones's key role in organizing the club and designing the course, and the continuing impact of the Masters is to me the most eloquent section of the book. He writes of those Masters regulars who say, "I'll meet you under the tree". The tree is the larger and more centrally located of the two huge, handsome, two-hundred-and-fifty-year-old live oaks on the terrace to the rear of the clubhouse. The terrace commands a majestic view of the golf course, which tumbles gradually down the huge natural amphitheatre to Rae's Creek. When someone at the Masters says to you, "I'll meet you under the tree," it's like wearing your first high heels.

Al writes at length about courage: of young Ouimet attacking down the stretch in his playoff with Vardon and Ray; of Hogan coming back after his accident; of Venturi struggling to keep going on the last day of the 1964 Open; and so on. He includes affecting descriptions of grace in defeat that old friends of his had demonstrated—Glenna Collett Vare, Lloyd Mangrum, and Arnold Palmer, among others. His understanding of people gave me an insight into the lessons golf teaches.

"Following the Leaders" reiterates the old assertion that golf helps to develop problem solvers not only on the golf course, but in other sports, in business and the sciences. The people in Al Laney's world would be achievers in any level of society. His book presents life and golf on many levels. I find it a joy. It was exactly the vehicle he needed to reassemble the persons who meant the world to him. I can wish no more for Al than his description of Muirfield in 1929: "The air had wine in it, the water was full of white caps and white sails, and the larks were actually singing." I hope when I go they're still singing and Al's there.

Carol McCue